PARENTS AND SCHOOLS:
PARTNERS OR PROTAGONISTS?

D1340172

PARENTS AND SCHOOLS:
PARTNERS OR PROTAGONISTS?

Gill Crozier

Trentham Books

Stoke on Trent, UK and Sterling, USA

Trentham Books Limited

Westview House	22883 Quicksilver Drive
734 London Road	Sterling
Oakhill	VA 20166-2012
Stoke on Trent	USA
Staffordshire	
England ST4 5NP	

© 2000 Gill Crozier

First published 2000

British Library Cataloguing-in-Publication Data
A catalogue record for this book is available from the British Library

1 85856 146 9 (paperback)

Designed and typeset by Trentham Print Design Ltd., Chester and printed in Great Britain by Cromwell Press Ltd., Wiltshire.

Contents

Acknowledgements

I would like to express my sincere gratitude to all of the participants in the research: the parents; the teachers and senior managers from both Brightside and Acre Lane Schools for their willingness to be interviewed, their generosity in giving me their time in their very busy schedules; and also to the senior managers for helping me to organise interviews with teachers. I would like to thank the school students from Lowlands School for their time in giving the interviews; the teachers from Lowlands School for their support of the research and for tolerating any disruption caused and Mr S for his help in organising the interviews.

My deep felt thanks go to: Jason Pegg who worked on the 'parents' phase of the project and carried out many of the interviews, transcribed some of them and entered masses of questionnaire data onto the data base; and to Siobhan Wilson for helping me to carry out the interviews with the school students. I am also very grateful to Christine Flenley who transcribed most of the interviews with parents and all of the teachers' interviews and to Sue Hawkins who transcribed the school student interviews.

The funding for the research upon which the book is based came from funds deriving from the Research Assessment Exercise, and without that such an extensive piece of work would not have been possible. I am most grateful therefore to the Faculty of Education and Human Sciences at Bath Spa University College for supporting my research.

I am also extremely grateful to many colleagues and friends, and my family for their support and encouragement to get the book completed, and to colleagues, and students for the various discussions that we had around the issues dealt with in the book which helped me to develop my thinking. I would like to give a special mention to my son, Musembi Salandy who has been so encouraging; Christine Eden, Assistant Dean of the Faculty of Education and Human Sciences, at Bath Spa University College, for her support; Miriam David; David James; Diane Reay; Carol Vincent and Kay Wood for reading chapters for me and providing me with some much needed constructive criticism and insightful comments. Of course my interpretation of these and my use or misuse of them are entirely my own responsibility.

Chapters 3, 4 and 5 draw on data from and develop the arguments presented in the following previously published work Empowering the Powerful. *British Journal of Sociology of Education* 1997 18:2, Parents and Schools: partnership or surveillance? *Journal of Educational Policy* 1998 13:1, Is It a Case of 'We know when we're not wanted?' The Parents' Perception of Parent-Teacher Roles and Relationships. Educational Research, 1999 41:3, and Parental Involvement: who wants it? *International Studies in Sociology of Education* 1999 9:2.

Chapter 6 is a development of a paper originally presented to the Annual Conference of the British Educational Research Association at the University of Sussex 1999. It also incorporates questionnaire data and their discussion from Parental Involvement: who wants it? *International Studies in Sociology of Education* 1999 9:2.

To my mother, Norah Crozier and the memory of my father,
Norman Crozier

Introduction

As the inexorable juggernaut[1] of educational policy changes continues, the focus on parents remains unabated. Parents have become as important for New Labour as they were for the previous Conservative government. They were important in operationalising the quasi-marketisation of education under Thatcherism (Crozier, 1998); they are now particularly important in New Labour's attempts to drive up standards. Whether parents like it or not and whether teachers like it or not, parents are part of, even central to, the education strategy. Partnership is as much a watchword for this government as it was for the previous one. It would appear to be an indicator of the desire for inclusivity in the educational endeavour. Included in this, however, is a need for *commitment* by everyone. As the Secretary of State for Education, David Blunkett, said in the foreword to the White Paper *Excellence in Schools* (DfEE, 1997a):

> Partnership for change means commitment from everyone: from the family and the wider community; from those working in the education service; and from those who support it ... Everyone has a part to play ... (p.3)
>
> ... Parents are a child's primary educators and our partnership approach will involve them fully ... (p.12)

In the White Paper, parental involvement seems to have three meanings: one is about helping children improve their literacy and numeracy – this applies to the primary school; the second is about disciplining and improving the children's school attendance this seems to relate more to secondary schools; and the third is about giving parents 'a greater say in the way schools are run' (p.55), through representation on the school governing bodies and as parent governor representatives on LEA education committees. Underpinning this latter role, it is suggested, is the parents' part in calling teachers to account.

The current parental involvement discourse asserts unproblematically that parental involvement is 'a good thing'. The argument presented here examines this assumption and subsequently demonstrates that parental involvement is a more diverse, complex concept than is generally acknowledged and that its achievement is neither possible nor desirable in the same ways by all concerned. Parental involvement is thus shown to be multifaceted, interpreted differently by different constituents, and serving a variety of purposes at different times (Crozier, 1999b). Parents and teachers and indeed the school students themselves all have their own views on the nature of 'parental involvement' and what they want or do not want this to be – views which sometimes do not match with each other or indeed with the government's viewpoint either.

The model of parental involvement most often propounded is that of the white middle-class mother who has unlimited time to support her primary-aged child's reading, number work or other 'homework' activity. This white middle-class primary school model does not transfer to the secondary school, or to the lives of those mothers, especially lone mothers who are now being pressured into taking employment, or to those mothers who already have employment and more than one child; nor does it easily transfer to the 'becoming' young adults who occupy the secondary school and want independence from, not increased dependence on, their parents. Moreover, whilst it may more readily apply to the white middle-class mother, Walkerdine and Lucey (1989) remind us that this group of women are also oppressed by the demands on them to perform according to the normative view of the 'good' parent (Sharp and Green, 1975, Jowett and Baginsky, 1991 and Vincent, 1996). As they say, 'Middle class mothers had to make every minute of the day into a pedagogy so that they actually salvaged less time for themselves ...'(p.8).

Therefore, whilst parents are seen and treated as a homogeneous group, this is not the case. Parents comprise people from diverse groups living and working in diverse situations and family structures, and their diversity influences their relationship to the school. Also, with respect to educational involvement, parents usually means in practice, mothers, who are the most educationally active parents (David, 1993a; Reay, 1998).

Parents have been criticised both explicitly by the Secretary of State for Education for being 'lazy' or for '[disengaging] from their children's education' (reported in Carvel, 1998), and implicitly, for not fulfilling their responsibilities – as would seem to be the case with the instigation of home-school agreements (DfEE, 1998a) which require (although this is not legally enforceable) parents (and their children) to sign an agreement to fulfil certain requirements and abide by school rules. There is an assumption that where parents are not 'involved' or are not fulfilling their 'responsibilities' then it is the parents who are to blame. There has been little consideration by policy-makers of the relationship between parents and schools and the influences or potential influences upon parental involvement. Similarly much of the research into parental involvement in Britain has been focused upon the 'how to do it' issues (see for example Bastiani, 1989, Macbeth, 1989, Merttens and Vass, 1993, Topping, 1996, Wolfendale, 1992). The exceptions to this include Tomlinson's (1991 and 1992) work with parents from minority ethnic groups in which she looked at various constraints upon their involvement, and aspects of their relationships, with the school; and the various studies on school choice, including Adler *et al.* (1989), Coldron and Boulton (1991) Gewirtz *et al.* (1995), Thomas and Dennison (1991); and the studies of parent-school relationships by Reay (1998) and Vincent (1996) in Britain, Lareau (1989) in the USA and Connell *et al.* (1982) in Australia. These latter studies, except for Connell *et al.*, were carried out in primary (elementary in the USA) schools.

The purpose of my study was to look at the relationship between parents and their children's secondary school and to consider the nature of this in the light of parental involvement and parent-school partnership discourses. Lareau comments that sociologists of education tend to be preoccupied with the dynamics within rather than between institutions. Following her (together with Vincent, Reay and to some extent Connell *et al.*) I explore the problems and possibilities of parental involvement, the influences upon parents' behaviour, and attitudes towards involvement. This exploration is located within the policy context of 'responsibilisation', 'normalisation' and school/teacher accountability.

The book is based therefore upon a research project that focused on parent-school/teacher relationships. The parents and teachers were drawn from two local education authority (LEA) comprehensive, co-educational schools, in two cities in the UK. One of the schools (which I call Brightside) had a predominantly middle-class intake, and the other school (known here as Acre Lane) had a predominantly working-class intake. Further details of the schools are expounded in Chapter 2. In addition to addressing the views of parents and teachers, the views of students, another group frequently ignored in parental involvement discourse, have also been considered. These students were accessed through a third school, also LEA maintained, coeducational, and with a similar class composition to Acre Lane. This third school is known here as Lowlands School (further details of this school are given in Appendix 1).

Research methods

All parents at Brightside and Acre Lane who had children in years 7, 9 and 11 were initially sent a questionnaire. The purpose of this was to gather some background information about issues of choice of school, school-home communications and parental attitudes – how 'happy', for example, they were with the school. This information has been drawn on intermittently throughout the analysis presented here. It sometimes serves to validate some of the interview data by triangulation, and sometimes to present a broader picture of some of the issues. A key purpose of the questionnaire, however, was as a means of gaining access to parents. It provided us with the opportunity to introduce the research and ourselves, and it was through the questionnaire that parents were asked if they would be willing to be contacted for a follow-up interview. We did not ask respondents in the questionnaire for personal details, and so we were not at this point able to categorise the participants by social class. The interview participants were thus selected randomly from those who agreed to be approached. A total of 95 per cent (of the questionnaire respondents) agreed to be interviewed. Details of the questionnaire returns and the numbers and types of respondents selected for interview are given in Tables 1, 2, 3a and 3b.

A broadly interpretivist paradigm was employed, based on the premise of seeking an understanding of the actors' meanings whilst recognising that these are located within a wider socio-political context. In addition to the questionnaire, a semi-structured interview was used. The interviews with parents lasted approximately one to one and a half hours and in all cases except for three were tape-recorded. As can be seen from Tables 2 and 3 the majority of respondents were mothers. This is in keeping with others' research findings (see for example David *et al.*, 1994). We did not specify who we wanted to interview. Some parents chose to be interviewed together and some fathers also chose to be interviewed alone. The majority of these fathers were middle class (see Table 3b). Some fathers were present in the home when the interview was carried out but chose not to participate. When asked if the father

Table I Distribution of questionnaires[2] and numbers returned

Brightside	Year 7 N= 167	Year 9 N= 165	Year11 N= 159	Total returned:
N=491	49% (81)	52% (85)	41% (65)	47% (231)
Acre Lane	Year 7 N=311	Year 9 N= 340	Year 11 N=302	34% (323)
N=953	32% (99)	35% (118)	35% (106)	

Table 2 Who completed the questionnaire

	Mother	Father	Both	No Reply
Brightside	28%	5%	3%	64%
Acre Lane	22%	4%	2%	72%

Table 3a Gender of interview respondents

	Households	Parents	Mothers	Fathers	Couples
Brightside	57	63	49	14	6
Acre Lane	58	67	50	17	9

Table 3b Social class of interview respondents

	Middle-class households	Working class households	Middle-class fathers interviewed alone	Working-class fathers interviewed alone
Brightside	46	11	8	0
Acre Lane	16	42	4	3

was going to participate in the interview, the mother most frequently replied, for example, 'Oh he leaves this sort of thing to me.' Parents also chose the location for the interview. Most interviews were carried out in their home; one was carried out in a bookshop owned by the parent.

At Brightside fourteen teachers were interviewed, including the head teacher, one deputy head teacher, five heads of department, the heads of key stage 3 and key stage 4, three heads of year, group tutors and class-room teachers. At Acre Lane fifteen teachers were interviewed including a deputy head teacher and four heads of department, two heads of year, the heads of key stage 3 and key stage 4 and the 'sixth form', group tutors and classroom teachers. The chair of governors and three parent governors were interviewed from Brightside and the chair of governors and two parent governors from Acre Lane.

In addition 474 students from the third comprehensive school, Low-lands, were sent a questionnaire and at a later date 68 students were interviewed, to ascertain their views on their parents' involvement in their schooling. Details of these interviews are provided in Appendix 2.

Anonymity of schools and respondents has been safeguarded and all names have been changed.

Data analysis

The questionnaire data were analysed by means of the software package SNAP. The semi-structured interview data were analysed according to the principles of grounded theory introduced by Glaser and Strauss (1967) and subsequently developed by Strauss and Corbin (1990). Issues were thus identified through which patterns emerged and were subsequently categorised. These were cross-referenced and further analysed against each other and the literature. Some categories were discarded and those remaining form the body of this book. Quotations in the text represent examples of the issues that make up the categories.

'Race', gender and class in parent-school relations

As I have already said parents are not a homogeneous group. In this study they comprise broadly mothers and fathers from middle-class and working-class backgrounds. Few parents and their children were from minority ethnic groups; neither school had more than two per cent of children from these groups. Only three mothers from minority ethnic groups were interviewed (two from Brightside and one from Acre Lane) and two white mothers of 'mixed race' children, (one from Brightside and one from Acre Lane); consequently this does not feature as an explanatory category here.

However, gender and social class are particularly significant in terms of understanding the parent-school relationships in this study. Both of these dimensions had a bearing upon parents' material conditions which affected their ability or not to engage in this relationship and in turn this affected the ways in which they were perceived and responded to. As already indicated the majority of the respondents in this study were mothers, and they are the most active parents too. Consequently the demands on parents are in effect demands on mothers and likewise the criticisms of parents are mainly criticisms of mothers.

Moreover, as Reay (1998) and Smith (1988) for example have discussed, the work of mothers particularly in relation to their children's education, is frequently ignored and rendered invisible, notably in the absence of analyses of mothering work in academic research. When women are included as Reay (1998) points out, it is most often the experiences of white middle-class mothers who are presented as the norm.

Central to understanding the nature of the parent-school relationship and the influences upon it is the issue of social-class. The social class dimension emerged in this study as a major factor in its impact upon the attitudes of teachers towards the parents and the confidence and knowledge that the parents had or did not have in intervening on their child's behalf or becoming involved in other ways. This is, of course, not surprising since, as Reay (1998) states, 'there is a long history of sociological writing which positions the educational system as instrumental in the distribution of social disadvantage within society' (p.1).

Definitions of social class are, as we know, problematic. For the purpose of this research we gathered data on the parents' occupations and used the Goldthorpe and Hope (1978) and Goldthorpe (1987) categories to locate these in social-class terms. We also gathered data on parents' own education, qualifications and home occupancy status. These data have been used to validate our interpretations of the class significance of their occupation and to provide a broader picture of parents' backgrounds in order to help us to gain insight into their understanding of, familiarity with and confidence in educational processes: indeed, to gain insight into their cultural capital (Bourdieu and Passeron, 1977). I have subsequently allocated parents to the two broad groups of middle class and working class.

Goldthorpe and Hope's category III presented particular problems. The category does not differentiate between different levels of clerical jobs and secretarial work some of which might require quite sophisticated levels of Information and Communications Technology (ICT) skills for example, nor does it distinguish between a skilled secretary and an unskilled shop assistant. Most of the women respondents fell into category III and since most of these women did low paid, unskilled, often temporary, insecure or part-time jobs, I have included this category under the term 'working class'. There are some exceptions to this which are indicated in Appendix 3. In order for the reader to make a judgement for herself/himself I have put as much information as possible about the respondents who appear in the text into Appendix 3.

Also I have given respondents names in order to enhance the narrative and to indicate their gender. After each parent quotation I have indicated their social class, together with their child's school year and which school their child attended. In most cases parents had more than one child at the school. This is indicated in Appendix 3. Following Fine (1997) I have used the term 'parent' to denote both parents and guardians.

Structure of the book

The educational reforms that have taken place over the past decade and a half and have shaped and continue to shape the education system today have also served to reposition parents and teachers in relation to each other and the education of the children. In Chapter 1 some of the key policy changes that have been instrumental in doing this are set out and their implications for parent-school/teacher relationships are discussed. It is argued that this relationship is primarily underpinned by 'responsibilisation' of parents and teacher/school accountability. The parent-school/teacher relationship is thus seen as part of a process of normalisation and mutual surveillance.

In Chapter 2 details of the two case-study schools are presented. Included are details of the nature of the parent-school relationships at the time of the research, in terms of the schools' procedures for relating to the parents, keeping them informed and involving them in various activities. The chapter also identifies similarities and differences between the two schools in their relationships with and management of the parents.

Chapter 3 presents the nature of parental involvement according to the parents themselves; the teachers' expectations of the parents are also outlined. It is shown that parents have diverse views and practices regarding involvement, which in many cases do not match those of the teachers. The manifestation of differences is indicative of the different social-class locations which the parents occupy. Middle-class parents are much more visible than working-class parents in their relations with the school. Although, as will be shown, working-class parents are just as supportive of their children's education as middle-class parents, their 'invisibility' is perceived by teachers as indifference.

In Chapter 4 I look at the different influences upon parental involvement and the relationships parents have with the teachers. Issues discussed include those relating to school-parent communication, educational knowledge, reliance on the teacher, marginalisation, social capital and time and other commitments.

Chapter 5 presents the views of the teachers on parental involvement, together with the implications of parents' involvement for their professionalism, as they see this.

This is followed by the presentation in Chapter 6 of the students' views on parental involvement. As already explained, these students' views are not triangulated with those of the parents in the rest of the study. However, in many ways what they say reinforces what the parents from the other two schools said about their involvement and the factors influencing it. For these mainly working-class students, aspects of their relationship with the school also reflect the relationship between the working-class parents and the teachers.

Chapter 7 draws together the various strands of the book and develops the analysis in relation to issues of resistance and trust, finally identifying the need for a form of parental involvement underpinned by participatory and democratic practices.

Notes

1 Giddens (1991) also uses this metaphor but he uses it to discuss the unstoppable changes taking place with respect to modernity.

2 All numbers have been rounded up or down to the nearest whole number.

Chapter 1

Education policy and the repositioning of parents and teachers

Introduction

Concern about the fragmentation or breakdown of the traditional family structure gave rise to the preoccupation of the previous Conservative government with the family throughout the 1980s and into the 1990s (Lister, 1996; David, 1998). This putative breakdown of the traditional family was blamed for a series of social problems which led to the drive for 'back to basics' and the implementation of a succession of economic and judicial measures under the guise of achieving this. As Jagger and Wright (1999) say 'one of the most salient themes in the family values debates is the notion of crisis' (p.10). With the coming to power of New Labour the attack upon the family and lone parents (mothers) in particular, endured. Just like the Conservatives before them, New Labour continued to place parents centre stage in terms of their education and social policies.

This chapter is therefore concerned with the implications of these policies for parents and teachers, and their impact upon this relationship. In particular, the chapter is concerned with the element of expectations upon parents and the way schools are driven by the policy agenda to involve parents more fully than they ever have before. It is argued that as a result of these changes parents and teachers are repositioned in relation to each other, the school and the students, in a way that has been beyond their control. A backdrop or policy context is presented against which the subsequent report of parent-school relationships in the two study schools will be discussed. It should be borne in mind that some of the policies have been developed since the completion of the

1

empirical research. However, it is argued that these have done little to improve the relationship or the possibilities for developing it, but if anything have reinforced the surveillance on all the key actors in this relationship.

Schools in the market place

Government policies, in Britain particularly since the 1988 Education Reform Act, have meant that schools have had to respond in a business-like way to the competitiveness between them (Levačić, 1995; Glatter *et al.*, 1997), driven on by parents' right to choose their child's school, league tables, target setting, and the monitoring of performance centrally, locally and at school level (Ozga, 2000). These policy changes have meant that schools and their practices are more transparent than ever before, and have served to intensify the external gaze. There has been a range of statutory requirements including the production of prospectuses, the issuing of at least one annual progress report per child and the publication of examination results, together with four-yearly inspections, which include the involvement of parents and the publication of a report; all of these have placed the school under the spotlight.

The pressure on schools to recognise that parents have a right to a voice and thereby to information, as well as ensuring their commitment to school values and mission, continues to increase, as for example with the recent Home-School Agreements Policy and the Homework Policy, instigated by statute that took effect in September 1999. Likewise there is pressure on the parents to comply with a particular way of relating to their children's schools, as these two recent policies, amongst other measures, will ensure.

Government policy, both recent and current, places parents in the role of client, and consumer, and increasingly monitor of their children's educational activity (such as homework) and behaviour. Implicitly, in their role as consumers, parents are also cast in the role of calling teachers to account. Explicitly, parents now have a potentially greater opportunity, through membership of the school governing body, to have a say in the decision-making process and management of the school. The power of parents rests on their ability to employ the option to exit (Hirschman, 1970) if they are dissatisfied with what is being provided by the school and also the possibility of having a voice (ibid.) through the setting up of committees and associations (Chubb and Moe, 1997) and through representation on governing bodies. The extent to which parents do have a voice and wish to use it is a key concern of this book and as Chubb and Moe, who are generally in favour of the educational market, themselves acknowledge, everyone has 'voice' but some people are 'well armed and organized' (p.365) to use it, whilst others are not. The market, then, has created a competitive arena not only for schools, but also for parents.

Parents as consumers

The crux of the Conservative government's policy on education was parental choice. This was designed to ensure the operationalisation of the market within the education system. Under the Conservatives a range of schools (LEA, CTC, GM, grammar schools, specialist schools, together with assisted places for the private sector) had been set up in order to ensure 'choice' and diversity.

The role of the school governors since the 1988 Education Act and Local Management of Schools (LMS) in particular has become of paramount importance. Whether parents have a real choice of school for their child and whether the increase of school governors' places for parents amounts to greater participation by parents is of course the subject of much debate and research (see for example Gewirtz et al., 1995 regarding the former; Deem et al., 1995 and Martin, 1999 regarding the latter). Be that as it may, as argued by Featherstone (1991) amongst others, we live in a consumer society and as a result society's citizens are increasingly having their expectations raised. The media have played an important part in this, with the publication of league tables both at national and local level, and the citing of failing schools or schools mentioned for example in the Chief Inspector for Schools' annual reports. Also, reporting of this information no longer remains solely the province of the broadsheets: the tabloids too are keen monitors of school performances. As Ozga (2000) has observed, 'Nearly two decades of consistent media and political criticism have established a media convention and public perception of inadequacy' (p.26).

Such changes were intended to establish the 'consumer' as the driving force in educational change (Woods, 1993). Parents tend not to describe themselves as consumers (see for example, Hughes *et al.*, 1994 and McClelland *et al.*, 1995). The provision of education, as others have noted too (for example, Walford, 1994), cannot be easily equated with the purchase and consumption of a product like a car or a television set. Parents are not themselves 'consuming' the education on offer but they are acting as consumers on behalf of their children, in so far as they are overseeing the accumulation of the 'product'. Their actions as consumers, within the context of the school, can be described as taking the form of questioning the actions and practices of the teacher, course content, policy decisions; organisational decisions and so on. In that sense they could be said to be 'over-seeing' the 'product-process' (Crozier, 1997).

Not all consumers though 'consume' from an equal position. Feather-stone identifies three main perspectives on consumer culture. The second of these he describes as follows:

> the satisfaction derived from goods relates to their socially structured access in a zero sum game in which satisfaction and status depend upon displaying and sustaining differences within conditions of inflation. The focus here is upon the different ways in which people use goods in order to create social bonds or distinctions. (1991, p.13)

This would seem to equate with the nature of this quasi-consumerism of parents. Brown (1997) describes parental consumerism as the ideo-logy of parentocracy and with it a shift away from the meritocratic system set in motion by the 1944 Education Act to one where the oppor-tunity to get a 'good' education lies with how 'powerful' the parents are, in the sense of being equipped with educational knowledge and the ability to act on it. Consumer culture operating within education acts to increase the power differential, rather than, as Featherstone suggests it might, as ' a process of functional democratization' (1991 p115). Con-sequently the rights of the consumer would seem to take priority over the rights of the citizen (Whitty, 1997a).

The role of parent as consumer is an essential part of the educational quasi-market (Le Grand and Bartlett, 1993); it is also part of the strategy to develop stakeholder Britain (Hutton, 1995) and to engage people in doing things for themselves; what I term 'self-helpism'. There are, I suggest, two related dimensions of self-helpism. One is concerned with developing an attitude towards and the practice of 'civic responsibilities' (Davies, 1993) based upon the maxim now adopted by New Labour of 'no rights without responsibilities' (Giddens, 1998). The other is a means of dealing with crises in the welfare state. Repeated financial cutbacks in education over the past twenty or more years, the effects of shifting employment opportunities due to globalisation and the changes in the employment of women (David, 1993a, Brannen *et al*, 1997) – what Giddens (1994) describes as 'social reflexivity'– have required the government to look at alternatives to supporting the education and health of the nation. With respect to the financial aspect, as Finch and Mason stated during the Conservative administration:

> It can be shown that, in periods when governments are trying to keep down costs of public expenditure, there is an incentive to encourage families to provide as much as possible. One such period, it can be argued, was the 1980s when the British and many other Western governments tried to re-draw the boundary between state responsibilities and family responsibilities to place more in the realm of the family. (1993, p.177)

Self-helpism is also facilitated by the information revolution and the accessibility to 'expert' knowledge. We've recently seen the introduction of an NHS web site designed to facilitate self-diagnosis, where people can access details of common illnesses and ailments. Prior to that the DfEE set up the National Grid for Learning and a web site providing an abundance of information about the Standard Assessment Tasks (SATs), OFSTED reports on schools, and league table details. In addition to this, it is very easy for parents to purchase their children's reading books and text books either from the local bookshop or again via the Internet. Such proliferation of information is intended to enable anyone to become an expert. This practice of accessing 'expert' knowledge is described by Rose (1990) as an attempt to acquire a form of personal freedom. In a later publication he goes on to say that '[t]he regulation of conduct becomes a matter of each individual's desire to govern their own conduct freely in the service of the maximization of a version of their happiness and fulfilment ... Individuals are to become their 'experts of themselves'' (Rose, 1996, p.59). Once they are 'the experts' of course, they then become responsible for their own actions.

Hence such empowered and informed parents should be able to ensure that their children succeed within the educational system.

Responsibilisation

The development of citizen-expertise and the appropriation of professional knowledge by individual citizens may constitute a reversal of power relations, at least in the sense of empowering citizens to call the professional to account, in principle enabling them to exert some influence; but as 'no rights without responsibilities' suggests, this has implications of accountability for the individual citizen too. In his article 'Governing Advanced Liberal Democracies', Rose (1996) writes of the historical development of responsibilisation of citizens as a political strategy of government at a distance. Since the inception of the welfare state he argues, this strategy has been employed particularly with 'incapable' or 'aberrant members of society' (p.49). Through the marketisation of education and the promotion of individualism, a fragmented system has emerged which also requires some form of management and control (Crozier, 1998). Parents are harnessed to bring this about through their desire to protect their own interests, in this case the perceived needs of their children. This requirement is acknowledged in the White Paper of 1992 'The corollary of increased autonomy [such as through Local Management of Schools] is greater accountability by them [the teachers] to parents, employers and the wider community' (DfEE, 1992, p.4).

The strategy of responsibilisation has thus been evoked once again but it also takes on an additional form. I have described this elsewhere (Crozier, 1998), drawing on Foucault (1977), as the inculcation of disciplinary power. Hence, rather than imposing overt punishment or sanctions in order to seek compliance and the 'reproduction of systems of rule' (Dandeker, 1990, p.37), tutelage is employed which develops a form of self-surveillance and self-discipline; but this has to be based upon that which is accepted, in other words it requires a process of normalisation. This is similar to Donzelot's (1979) view, in writing about a different historical period, that the state entrusts parents with the responsibility of providing both socially and morally developed young people and does so through indirect means and yet has a 'ubiquitous presence acting as both guarantor and deterrent, posing ultimately as an ever present threat to those on the margins' (Wyness, 1997, p.312). The signing of the home-school agreement can be seen as an example of this. If disciplinary power works well and parents behave as responsible citizens, they will both want and see it as their duty to sign the agreement. Giddens (1994) in talking about the 'Third World' makes comparisons between aid and the welfare state in industrialised societies. He discusses the importance of self-reliance arguing that 'responsibility closely accords with self-reliance' (p.162), or self-helpism in my terms, and claims that where aid does not require reciprocity then dependency can ensue.

The policies in relation to parents and schools are therefore two-pronged: firstly to create a structure whereby parents monitor the teachers' work and call them to account and secondly to ensure that parents take on their own 'responsibilities'. In these respects there is little difference between the policies of the Conservative and New Labour governments. Whitty *et al.* (1998) have asserted that under New Labour there has been a shift from parental rights to parental responsibilities. Notwithstanding my point concerning the introduction of home-school agreements, it is my view that this comprises a shift in emphasis rather than a change in policy. The Conservatives were as keen to 'bind' parents in (as Gillian Shepherd, the then Secretary of State for Education, put it) to the process of education and the values of the school (see Crozier, 1998) as they were to ensure the surveillance of teachers through parental choice and the right of parents to exert 'exit and voice' (Hirschman, 1970) if they were not satisfied.

In their bid to drive up standards and address the issue of social exclusion, New Labour have also sought ways of binding – in parents and ensuring that they take on their responsibilities. In addition to a number of judicial measures with respect to parents having to take responsibility for their children's repeated unofficial absences from school (Home Office, 1997a), New Labour have been critical of parents' commitment to their children's education in general and their ability to look after them properly, and have laid (at least) partial blame at their door for children's poor educational performance as well as poor behaviour. (The rest of the blame was laid squarely on the teachers according to the Chief Inspector for Schools in his annual reports, for example, Woodhead, 1998, 2000.) At a conference in the spring of 1998 David Blunkett, Secretary of State for Education, was reported as saying:

> When there is a problem it is all too often because parents claim not to have the time, because they have disengaged from their children's education or because ...they lack even the basic parenting skills... So far from being a nanny state, we must become an enabling state, which ensures that parents and families have the backing when they need it. (Carvel, 1998)

As well as pathologising parents, this statement homogenises them as though they all behave in the same way and indeed have the same material opportunities to behave in the same way. It also embodies an ideology that there is a 'right' way of parenting. As David (1999) says 'the Government has adopted ... an inclusive definition of families and parents [with the intention of] ... prescribing and planning to regulate parental standards for all' (p.218). Blunkett's solution to the problems he outlines above was to set up classes for parents to learn how to support their children's development of literacy and numeracy and to require school governors to draw up home-school agreements, first proposed by the previous Conservative government. These agreements, as stated above, became a statutory requirement by September 1999. Around the same time the Home Secretary, Jack Straw, introduced the measure whereby parents of children who had offended may be required to undergo parenting classes if their parenting competence was in doubt (Carvel, 1998). In actual fact these classes are targeted at mothers, who have traditionally been held responsible for their children's behaviour and social development in general (Harris, 1983), and 'particular groups of needy families, largely lone mothers living in particularly poor localities' (David, 1999, p.220).

These policy developments also ignore what parents do in the home in relation to their children's support and development. As Duncan and Edwards (1998) argue, these activities include emotional work and educational work. Increasingly with government policy interventions and the expectations thus imposed upon parents, the boundary between home and school is being blurred and the home is steadily being transformed into an educational setting (Edwards and Alldred, 1998). One of the consequences of these changes in education and home-school relations is the increased burden upon mothers (David, 1998; Smith, 1998). Whilst various policy initiatives are invoked requiring the family or parents to comply, little support is forthcoming to enable parents to take greater responsibility or participate more fully (Lister, 1996). The converse is in fact the case with the increased pressure on lone parents to take paid employment, and the failure of successive governments to ensure paid parental leave.

Getting the right parents

Unlike other consumers, the type of parent consumer is important (Ball, 1994). If parents are to play a key role in ensuring the smooth running of our diverse education system, and indeed to operate as responsible citizens, then their 'normalisation' must be assured. Ways in which this can be demonstrated at policy level include the Home-School Agreements Policy (DfEE, 1998a), and the Homework Policy (DfEE, 1998b) which as David (1999) has argued brings home-school relations into the public gaze and increases opportunities for surveillance and control of parents' activities as much as those of their children.

Normalising parents also becomes important from the perspective of the schools. Not only do they want compliant parents who support them in their endeavours and parents who support their children, but they also want parents who can contribute to the overall well-being of the school, for example in relation to the school governors. Since LMS (Local Management of Schools), the role of the school governors has become paramount, with responsibility for economic and administrative concerns and to a lesser extent for curriculum matters as well (Bullock and Thomas, 1997). As Whitty *et al.* (1998) suggest, the desirability of some parents as governors is therefore greater than others, and 'It would seem that the most socially advantaged schools will also be able to draw on more expertise from their communities' (p.107). Deem *et al.* (1995) and Thomas and Martin (1996) found that working-class and minority ethnic group parents were under-represented on governing bodies. Consequently Whitty *et al.* (1998) go on to say that the market and the need to meet government objectives are potentially leading to the commodification of parents as well as students (p.95). Although the signing of home-school agreements is not compulsory, any parent who refuses to do so will be signalling themselves as a potential problem for the school. Whilst schools are not supposed to make the signing a condition of entry, given that secondary schools can now select up to 15 per cent of their students, it leaves open the possibility of operating this as an implicit selection criterion. Macleod (1996) suggests that home-school agreements are also about 'ensuring that parents have the right disposition towards school policies such as discipline and homework' (quoted in Whitty *et al.*, 1998, p.105).

A 'good' parent is one who is obedient, one who 'behaves in a particular way in school' (Vincent, 1996), according to the desires of the teacher. A 'good' parent also fulfils that role out of school, to ensure ' organised learning out of school' (Barber, 1996, p.266). As Barber says:

> Many thousands of children and young people participate in organised learning out of school. They take part in Cubs and Brownies, the Scouts and Guides. They attend dance lessons and music lessons. They ride horses and go swimming ... The children and young people who benefit from this range of activities only do so because their parents have the will and the means. They seek out the opportunities, they commit the time and energy and where it is required, they stump up the necessary cash. These parents, the ones who make the effort and, if they have it, provide the funding, are good parents. (p.266-7)

Whilst he does acknowledge that some parents do not have the 'cash' to do the things he values as 'organised learning out of school', the implication nevertheless is that they conversely are 'bad' parents. His intention here though is not just to criticise, but rather to promote a strategy, in this case 'the Individual Learning Promise', to achieve normalisation.

The purpose of getting 'the right parent' could be seen in terms of what Donzelot refers to as 'the transition from a government of families to a government through the family' (1979, p.92).

Schools, teachers and the market: teachers under surveillance

Getting the 'right' parent usually means getting the powerful parent, which is not always so desirable for the classroom teacher even if it suits the senior management of the school. Moreover, getting the 'right kind' of parent can be used to get the 'right kind' of teacher or at least to fashion teachers into 'the right kind'. Writing in the 1980s about teacher-parent relationships in Australia, Elizabeth Hatton (1985) described the power of certain parents to choose 'the right kind' of teacher as far as they were concerned and their ability to get what they wanted. The powerful parent in Hatton's case study was in fact able to ensure that certain teachers were dismissed and that others were or were not appointed. Through the power of the governing body in England and Wales and the increased representation of parents on the school governing body this in theory would also be possible here. School governors are responsible for the hiring and firing of staff, although traditionally they have deferred to the head teacher and the link LEA adviser.

The point at issue here is the increased control over teachers. This can also be seen in relation to teacher appraisal and the (as yet unrelated) planned introduction of performance-related pay (DfEE, 1998c) based upon student achievement and progress. Performance-related pay will be based on whether or not teachers have satisfactorily implemented the National Curriculum, and/or the literacy and numeracy hours. The Advanced Skills Teacher Scheme (DfEE, 1998c) whereby 'successful', 'achieving' teachers will be rewarded, is another initiative with the same controlling intentions. These incentives and promotional devices could be interpreted as constraints upon teachers voicing objections to policy developments and indeed putting into practice anything that deviates from the dominant ideology within current policy. As Ozga (2000) argues, teachers are under pressure to succeed; 'they are in competition with each other and with other schools' (p.21). Indeed it could be said that there is a policy of normalisation of teachers too, as well as of parents, whilst both parents and teachers are involved in the normalisation process of each other.

In her study of primary school relationships between parents and teachers, Vincent (1996) revealed divisions between parents and teachers which she characterised as the 'lay-professional' divide that was maintained on the basis of the teachers' ideal view of the 'good' parent, a role which parents can never live up to. Although the 'good' parent was a desirable parent from the teachers' perspective, 'the good' parent was the 'supportive' but not the 'interfering' parent. Whilst this is frustrating for parents, Whitty et al. (1998) remind us that although teachers may be inclined to protect their own vested interest, it must also be recognised that they too are 'struggling to find some sort of voice within the continual wave of reforms' (p.107).

The reforms have in many ways shown disregard for teachers and for their professionalism in general (Hargreaves, 1994). This, coupled with overt criticisms by ministers and government representatives, has had a demoralising effect on the profession (Gewirtz, 1997). In addition, these remorseless changes have led to the intensification of teachers' work (Hargreaves, 1994) resulting in many cases of stress (Kyriacou, 1998) and teacher 'burn-out' (Leithwood et al., 1996).

It has also been argued that the changes in the education system over the past fifteen to twenty years have systematically undermined teachers' professionalism, particularly in relation to curriculum autonomy and more recently with respect to their pedagogy and the routinisation of their work, the demise of their decision-making power and in effect their deskilling (Hargreaves, 1994; Apple, 1988). The consequences of this have been described as the proletarianisation of teaching (Lawn and Ozga, 1988; Robertson, 1996).

Bowe et al. (1992) point to the tension that has arisen for teachers between the 'traditional teacher professionalism and the forces of the market as criteria for educational decision-making' (p.51). They highlight the dissatisfaction that teachers feel about this and the need to engage in practices which have more resonance with the world of business and finance than with the school, the process of learning and the orientation of a caring profession. An essential aspect of this is Local Management of Schools. Whether LMS has led to an improvement in effective management and ultimately in children's learning remains unclear, but there are strong indications that the consequences of the management styles adopted and the imperatives imposed by LMS have led, in some cases at least, to a separation between classroom teachers and senior management (Bullock and Thomas, 1997). And even though head teachers may, in one sense, be given greater autonomy with respect to resource decisions, as Bullock and Thomas highlight, they are now required to consult school governors on all decisions about human and physical resources and this too, in effect, constitutes a reduction in professional judgement.

Hoyle and John (1995) suggest that the development of accountability of the professionals (which they term 'the accountability movement') could be seen as arising from the ideology of the New Right. With respect to education, they list the following as an indication of some of the measures employed to ensure school/teacher accountability:

- increased power for governors
- Local Management of Schools
- grant maintained status
- open enrolment
- the National Curriculum
- Standard Assessment Tasks
- systematic inspection by OFSTED teams
- publication of inspection reports
- institutional development plans
- publication of school examination results and other data
- teacher appraisal (p.108)

To this could be added performance-related pay and the 'super teacher' incentives referred to above, and the introduction of teacher contracts. Hoyle and John (1995) also say that prior to the introduction of these accountability measures, there was a view that teachers were un-accountable. They argue that whilst this may have been the case, teachers' relative autonomy was matched by a high level of professional integrity and responsibility. In the light of this it is interesting to consider whether or not these systems of accountability have now or will in the future undermine teachers' sense of responsibility. Do these systems, together with the undermining of teachers' overall professionalism, lead to a passive somewhat dependent 'work force'? Ironically such an outcome would constitute that very dependency culture that Giddens (1994) cautions against with respect to society's citizens. Whilst this is speculative, what is clear from others' research already discussed is that teachers' professionalism has been undermined, resulting partly, *inter alia,* in their demoralisation.

A further consequence of the reforms has been the development of a 'market phase of school leadership' (Grace, 1995), or what others have described as the 'new managerialism' (Mahoney and Moos, 1998). The new managerialism is characterised by greater control over the labour process based upon economic rationalism (Codd, 1993), to ensure that the school has and maintains a competitive edge. However, Ball (1993) argues that the control of teachers under this new regime represents a more subtle form of control rather like the disciplinary power invoked over parents, referred to earlier. Drawing on Kickert's (1991) term of 'steering at a distance', he explains that through these various controlling measures teachers (like parents) are inculcated with the skills of self-monitoring. The new measures of performance-related pay and 'super teacher' status could be said to embody this.

All the control measures discussed in this chapter would seem to be two-pronged: they are both implicit and explicit, leaving nothing to chance. Hence, for teachers, teacher accountability and the bureaucratic arrangements under the new managerialism increase the visibility of their work and correspondingly intensify the external gaze, both aspects resulting in increased control (Giddens, 1984; Hargreaves, 1994).

Conclusion

Traditionally the school has been the domain of the teacher. The changes brought in by the Conservative government and developed by New Labour have shifted the orientation so that the parents' right to know is established through a range of requirements, and opportunities are established for them to have a greater say, potentially, in the education of their children. In effect teachers' authority has been challenged and they now find themselves in a situation in which they are more accountable. Not only is the 'secret garden' of the curriculum (Callaghan, 1976) opened up but so too is the whole 'estate' of the school and education system.

On the other hand, parents' rights have become coupled with their responsibilities, and a process of normalisation, together with one of mutual accountability and surveillance (between themselves and teachers) has been put in place. Whether this has created the conditions for a harmonised, productive partnership between parents and teachers or, conversely a situation of antagonistic relationships is the focus of the research study with which the rest of the book is concerned.

In the next chapter the two study schools and the general nature of the parent-school/teacher relationship will be presented and discussed.

Chapter 2

Parent-school relationships:
the case of two schools

Introduction

The purpose of this chapter is to present the broad details and nature of the parent-school relationships that existed at the time of the research in the two case-study schools, Brightside and Acre Lane. In doing so, it is also my intention to lay the ground for exploring the different roles and behaviours within the relationship, the influences upon these and the different perspectives on what is actually going on. In the recent past it was often reported that schools were not welcoming to parents and did little to encourage their involvement (Vincent, 1996; Wolfendale, 1992). Over the last ten to fifteen years this situation has changed markedly and schools now have little choice but to woo parents, at the very least in order to attract their 'custom'. Once the parent/child has made the choice of school, the school needs to ensure that the child remains on roll. Moreover, as Everard and Morris (1996) have pointed out, there is an imperative upon head teachers to actively develop and project a positive image of their school within the wider community and they need to 'solicit co-operation and support for their activities' (p.221) in this respect.

A clear focus for these intentions must be parents. As schools are required increasingly to meet a range of targets and performance indicators, from improved examination results to lowering rates of unapproved absences, the school needs to establish and activate the parents' commitment to and support for school values. As well as the external more visible image of the school, 'what the school is like' and 'what goes on in the school' are conveyed to parents, the children and the wider community through what Pollard (1985) terms 'institutional bias'. Pollard explains institutional bias as:

> A type of generally shared knowledge, a diffuse and often tacit set of social understandings or cultural assumptions about a school and about practices in it. These conventions are developed over time and frequently reflect the perspectives of those with most power and influence in the school. (p.116)

As Pollard also points out, institutional bias, although it usually becomes internalised into the routine of the school, is not static and can be influenced and changed. Whilst to discern fully the institutional bias of a school one would need to undertake an ethnographic study, the information presented here about the two study schools is intended to give a sense of this nevertheless, particularly with respect to parents and how they experienced the schools' attempts to relate to them.

Attention has already been drawn to the importance of viewing parents as heterogeneous and to the fact that mothers are the most active parents. Details will therefore be given of the gender of the parents at the two study schools together with their social class, given their importance as explanatory categories, discussed in the Introduction.

The case of two schools
Brightside
Brightside School had 950 students, 150 of these in the sixth form. It is a coeducational comprehensive school, located on the edge of Georgetown, a small prosperous city in a middle-class area. Brightside, according to the chair of the school governors, had a very good reputation. It was mentioned by OFSTED as one of 52 'good' schools and it was over subscribed. The children were drawn from a wide area throughout the city and surrounding areas. Those coming from the outlying areas tended to be from working-class families whilst those nearer to the school, the city dwellers, were more likely to be from middle-class backgrounds. In response to a question about his impression of the social class composition of the school, the head teacher replied that in his view 60 per cent of the parents were middle-class, many of these professionals, and some from social class C1; 40 per cent were working-class. In our sample of interviewed parents, slightly more parents represented the professional and intermediate classes. The school was predominantly white with approximately ten students from minority

ethnic groups. Only two parents (mothers) from minority ethnic groups participated in the research, as well as one white mother of a 'mixed race' child.

According to parents and teachers, parent-school relationships could be described as very positive at Brightside. In their questionnaire responses, the vast majority of parents said that they were either *very happy* (42 per cent) or *happy* (42 per cent) with the school. This view was borne out by the interview data from parents, and teachers too described relations with parents as 'good' and said that they welcomed parental 'involvement'. In the handbook given to all parents of children newly enrolled in the school, the importance of 'partnership' is emphasised in developing a 'successful education.' The handbook also stresses the value the school places upon contact with parents.

Details of syllabuses, examination details and so on were provided in a year booklet. Parents were given termly information about their child's progress by means of a grade card (the child received a grade for effort and a grade for achievement) and the statutory yearly written report provided more detailed information. Parents were also given the opportunity to make comments on the yearly report and in the child's homework diary. Details of homework tasks were recorded, in the homework diary, which parents were expected to sign on completion of the homework. There was a parents' consultation evening once a year, and over the child's time at the school there were occasional curriculum evenings. Nevertheless, there was some dissatisfaction hinted at in the questionnaire responses, with 55 per cent of respondents saying they were only *quite satisfied*, (although 42 per cent said they were *very satisfied*) with the information they received about their child's progress, and 69 per cent only *quite satisfied* with the information they received about what their children did in school. This point will be returned to in the next chapter.

A head teacher's newsletter was sent to parents twice monthly giving information about future meetings and reports of meetings that had taken place, health and safety issues, reminders on school policy regarding for example 'illegal substances', and details of letters that had been sent home in the previous two weeks. Parents did remark on the substantial amount of information that the school sent out to them, although not necessarily information that gave them details of their own child's progress and how they could provide support.

The questionnaire responses indicated that parents' evenings were *always* attended by 77 per cent of the parent respondents and 18 per cent said that they *sometimes* attended; 3 per cent said that they never attended and 2 per cent did not reply. The head teacher verified this response.

The Parent Teacher Association was active and it was described (in the handbook to new parents) as having 'the purpose of involving parents actively in the school and their children's education'. It would do this through three types of activity: social, educational and fund-raising.

When we interviewed the parents the majority of them spoke very highly of the school, particularly of its being approachable, having a caring ethos and being supportive of the students; and they said they felt that the school and the teachers were accessible. The teachers felt that the school and in most cases the parents were working together for the same things.

The school according to the staff had broken down barriers, and parents were encouraged to telephone teachers and talk about their concerns, so much so that a 'telephoning' culture had developed and even those parents who felt more on the margins said that if they needed to they would telephone the school about their concerns. Some parents were forever telephoning about something, and teachers too would telephone parents if necessary. Some teachers described the relationship as an 'easy' one between them and the parents. Parents reported that if they left messages the teachers would respond quickly. As this year 9 mother (Mrs Jones, social class university student, father social class II) explained:

> Whenever you phone up, I mean I've had to phone up sometimes in the morning, half past eight, or quarter to nine and they will go and get the teachers from the staff room...or they'll always take a message and give it to the teacher.

And a father (Mr Darby, year 11, social class II, mother social class II) said:

> There was a time when I felt he [his son] wasn't being given the right sort of work and I went into school then and discussed it with the teacher. And was impressed by the reception I got; the listening they did and the follow-up. I mean I know there's the facility for me to do that.

Another mother (Mrs Butler, year 9, social class I, father social class I) said:

> ... one of the things would be openness and accessibility; accessibility of the staff if you've got a query or a problem or anything...[they] have this system of leaving a message and ... I think without fail I've been rung back in break time or by the end of that day and I've found that impressive...

A year 11 mother (Mrs Foley, social class III, lone parent, father social class unknown):

> I think the friendliness, they put you at your ease. You know even if they were about to tell you horrible things ... I think sometimes parents can walk into parents' evenings and [the teacher says] 'your child has been abysmal, you must do this!' You feel as if you personally have done something wrong. I've never felt like that at [Brightside] ...They might have a problem but there's always a solution; there's always a solution to every problem.

Some parents said that the ethos of the school demonstrated the value placed on people and others spoke of the dedicated staff and positive relationships between staff and students as well as staff and parents. Such views tended to emanate from middle-class parents, although working-class parents, were also generally satisfied with the school. Working-class parents as will be seen, had a more distant relationship with the school and therefore tended to have fewer expectations than middle-class parents about the accessibility of the school; they tended to approach the school much less often than middle-class parents but did expect the school to keep them informed about their child's progress. In most cases and in general they were satisfied with this state of affairs.

At Brightside, the school governing body was unusually dominated by parents, many of whom had been co-opted deliberately in order that parents should hold a majority. They were also middle-class and were described as 'left wing' by some of the other parents, a view endorsed by the parent governors we interviewed. Overall the parent body comprised a powerful group whose social class and status in society gave them a potentially significant opportunity to have a voice and influence within the school. The powerful representation of parents on the governing body was another aspect of this. The requirement of the school to respond to market imperatives and parent pressure further enhances, this potential.

The head teacher, who had been at the school only two years prior to our research, was aware of this. As he said,

> That's where I feel it [that is, parental involvement] most powerfully in terms of you know the sort of professional class background of over half of the pupils, um – in that, I've now become used to it but to begin with I found it extremely demanding, the extent to which the parents, while wanting to be constructively critical, you know can be critical...

And, he went on,

> I think within the first three weeks here I received five critical letters about the curriculum, you know I'd never experienced a situation where I received four sides of A4 typed, you know, about year 9 options. (Quoted in Crozier, 1998)

He was particularly conscious of the ability and willingness of the parents to network and the possible consequences of this for him and the school. For example,

> You know there is a lot about the chattering classes, I mean [Georgetown] is a village really and people are [pause], you know, if I get something wrong, you know the dinner table talk, will, will you know...well your paper [a research report written for the school] showed that, I think it's the school's reputation that's come through there really loud and clear and in [Georgetown] a lot of that reputation is over the dinner table... (Quoted in Crozier, 1997)

An additional role that schools in contemporary Britain (and elsewhere) have now to play is dealing with parents who challenge the schools' decisions and with confrontational parents (as reported in Barnard, 1999). An essential aspect of this is being able to manage the parent-school relationship (Everard and Morris, 1996).

There was a contrast, however, between the presence and behaviour of middle-class parents and working-class parents and the impact of this on teachers' consciousness. At Brightside we only interviewed parents from eleven working-class households (as detailed in the Introduction), which is partly indicative of the low percentage of working-class families in the school. Whilst the active involvement of middle-class parents contributed to ensuring the school's attentiveness to their needs; the needs of working-class parents and children were not always or entirely the same. Overall the working class parents expressed satisfaction, but they also spoke of feeling marginalised, and of the various activities and committees as not being for them. Therefore whilst parents at Brightside were actively involved and there were strong school-parent links, these were dominated by middle-class parents.

In interviews with the teachers parents were rarely differentiated or characterised by social class but instead they were euphemistically referred to as the 'more/less articulate parents', 'the parents of the more motivated children' or 'the more motivated parents'. Working-class parents were in fact rarely referred to at all at Brightside, except in these somewhat disparaging terms and as 'not having done something' (such as not having turned up for a parents' evening or a meeting with a teacher). The chair of governors did comment that the governors, at some time, had had a discussion about getting working-class parents more involved but at the time of the research nothing arose from that. Working-class parents did not seem to present a major concern for the school.

Acre Lane

Acre Lane is also an 11–18 co-educational LEA-maintained comprehensive school. At the time of the research it had 1700 students on roll. These included approximately 160 sixth-form students. There were 110 teaching staff. Acre Lane was one of the largest comprehensive schools in the area, located on the outskirts of a major city. It drew its student intake mainly from two large local authority housing estates and some low cost owner-occupier areas. One of the deputy head teachers described the student intake as coming from a mainly working-class background, although there were some pupils from homes where parents had professional jobs or management related employment. This characterisation is reflected in the parents we interviewed; these comprised 72 per cent (of the households) from social classes III to VII (see the Introduction and Appendix 3 for further details). 17 per cent of the students were receiving free school meals, which gives an indication of those families on income support at that time. The ethnic composition of the school was mainly white, with only approximately 25 of all the students coming from minority ethnic group backgrounds (mainly of Asian origin, although some were of African-Caribbean origin). Only one parent (mother) of Asian origin was interviewed in our sample and one mother whose son was 'mixed race'.

Whilst relationships with parents were thought by the staff to be generally good, senior management were concerned about parent-school relationships, prompted in part by the disbanding of the Parent Teacher Association due to lack of support. Mr Ratcliffe, one of the deputy head teachers, expressed a view about the parent-school relationship that 'it seems to be very difficult to get parents involved in anything unless it's on 'need to know basis'.' This was echoed by other members of staff, both managers and classroom teachers. If the issue concerned their own child directly, for example, subject choice then they would get a good response but for anything of a more general nature there was very little response. This lack of response to general issues is not unusual; it was the same amongst parents at Brightside, and other researchers (McClelland *et al.*, 1995) have reported this to be the case too. However, the key difference lies in the dissonance (Lareau, 1989) there seemed to be between the parent and school. The relationship was functional rather than displaying any active participation on the part of the parents, in whatever form; and in comparison with the majority of parents at Brightside, there was not the same proactivity on the part of Acre Lane parents. By contrast they responded when contacted rather than intitiating the action themselves. Mr Ratcliffe summed this up: 'So our relationship is very business-like...it's not really a community ... a supportive community.'

In the questionnaire parents did indicate that they were *very happy* (37 per cent) or were *happy* (35 per cent) with the school (a quarter of the respondents said they were *happy with reservations*). Whilst the follow-up interviews indicated that this was an overall view, parents did have concerns and criticisms of various aspects of the school and its relationship to them, which will be discussed in later chapters.

Few parents got actively involved in attending meetings, fund-raising or social events. However, the school had a tradition of putting on concerts and plays in which many of the students were involved and parents were very supportive in attending these events. Also whilst a school-initiated barn dance did not attract any parents, when a group of parents organised a fashion show which involved some of the students, 100 parents attended.

The school held an annual parents' evening when parents received a copy of their child's progress report and met the teachers to discuss this. According to the questionnaire data 58 per cent of parents said that they *always* attended parents' evenings and 31 per cent said that they sometimes did. 10 per cent said that they *never* did so. If parents could not attend the parents' evening they were invited to make an alternative appointment. However, Clarke and Power (1998) reported that from their study into schools' reporting to parents 'for many parents particularly working class and ethnic minority parents, the idea of availing themselves of these [alternative arrangements] was daunting' (p.6) and therefore unlikely to happen.

Both student and parent were invited to make written comments on the report. There was also a system of 'spotlighting' which provided an assessment of the way children study and work. An assessment was made against criteria which included: 'the student starts the lesson prepared to work; the student listens attentively and acts upon instructions; the student copes with the majority of tasks; the student consistently does homework when set.' This assessment was carried out by the year tutor on a weekly basis and a termly report was sent home to parents. On the basis of this, parents were asked to negotiate an action plan for and with their child in order to bring about improvements. These are significant demands upon the parents. Perhaps unsurprisingly therefore, parental written feedback was said by the teachers to be variable. Just as at Brightside, parents at Acre Lane were also expected to sign the homework diary and could make a comment if they so wished.

If a child was having difficulties and the standard of their work had fallen then it was the responsibility of the year tutor to contact the parent rather than to wait for parents' evening. They were also planning to circulate parents' telephone numbers to faculties (subject departments) in order to make it easier for staff to contact them so that if a child did not turn up for a detention or the teacher of a particular subject was concerned about something, then they could telephone the parent.

The school circulated a twice-termly newsletter to parents, and heads of departments, or the heads of key stages, would write letters to parents regarding a specific event or issues. There was no school policy on parent-school relationships, although there were targets within the school development plan and the business plan about developing links with parents.

With regard to information about their child's progress 44 per cent of parents said they were *very satisfied* with the information they received but 51 per cent were only *quite satisfied* and 5 per cent were *dissatisfied*. Regarding information about their child's behaviour 48 per cent were *very satisfied*, 44 per cent were *quite satisfied* and 7 per cent were *dissatisfied*. Similarly to the parents at Brightside only 24 per cent were *very satisfied* with the information they received about what their child did in school, 60 per cent were *quite satisfied* and 13 per cent were *dissatisfied*.

Just as at Brightside the telephone was actively used to ensure parent-school links. However, in this instance, according to Mr Ratcliffe (one of the deputy head teachers), it was more the staff contacting the parents than the other way round. He explained that exceptions to this were of two sorts:

> You'll get two groups of parents who'll contact us...one will be the ones [for] who[m], you know, there's a real problem – a sort of low level problem...about their [son's/daughter's] coat's gone missing and nothing's been done to find it; or you know, they had an earring taken from PE – we get lots of contact along those lines. And very often that is a parent that's angry... And then you'll get some parents who'll contact – not very many – who are really very insistent on finding out information almost on a week to week basis about their child progressing in school and that will tend to be... you might call them [the] more sort of middle-class parent...

Within the period just prior to my research Acre Lane had begun to put in place strategies for improving the achievement levels of its GCSE students, particularly for its borderline candidates. These strategies included individual tutorials and target setting. In addition the school wanted and needed to develop its recruitment to the sixth form. Near to Acre Lane was situated a Sixth Form College – St Jude's – which was developing a good reputation for its teaching and examination successes. St Jude's was in direct competition with Acre Lane and indeed many of those students who wanted to go on to take A levels would go there rather than remain in the sixth form at Acre Lane. Acre Lane, however, according to Mr Ratcliffe, had another issue to tackle and that involved raising the aspirations of the parents and therefore of their children. As he explained, traditionally most of the school's parents had not furthered their education and so the school had 'to put a lot of effort into getting them [the parents] to 'think university'.' As part of this the school arranged regular visits to local and regional universities, bussing the students there and arranging introductory sessions. In the sixth-form teaching team, one member of staff was designated the higher education coordinator and given the job of promoting higher education. They also held a higher education evening every year for year 12 students and their parents. Whilst it was thought that the attitudes of the parents strongly influenced their children, Mr Ratcliffe emphasised that it was not that the parents were unsupportive or did not want their children to do well but rather 'it's not quite knowing the mechanics of those systems, they don't know themselves'.

This was an additional task for the school to take on but as well as 'getting them to think university', it was apparent that parents were perceived as having a range of cultural values and practices which differed from those of the school/teachers. Again as Mr Ratcliffe explained:

> Parents mostly do want their children to do their homework, but it surprises me how many, talking to the youngsters, are actually out of the house at night. ... I think the pattern possibly is: come home, grab a snack, rush homework, haven't got any, done a little bit: 'Can I go out now?' 'Well you've got to be in by 10pm.' It's surprising how many pupils [for whom] that's the norm ... Children don't seem to think it's the norm to have to stay in at night during the week.

In place of the Parent Teacher Association, the school introduced a Parents' Forum. This was organised and run by the senior management team. No other teachers were invited to these meetings. The meetings were organised around a theme which was advertised to the parents. According to the head of sixth form these tended not to be well attended by parents 'and therefore probably not a very representative turn-out'. The middle-class parents interviewed said that they welcomed this opportunity to meet and put forward their views, although they were still (at that time) reserving their judgement about how effective they would be in having any influence. As will be seen, whilst some working-class parents attended these meetings, those who we interviewed never went back a second time. They felt that the issues did not concern them or else that the way in which they were presented was exclusionary.

Nevertheless, most parents felt that the school was serving them and their children reasonably well and they were satisfied overall. There was a view that the teachers were usually approachable if parents needed to talk to them; but if there was no need then there was little contact. If the child was in difficulty then there was an assumption that they (the parents) would be contacted. As will be shown in Chapter 3 however, middle-class parents were more inclined to intervene on their child's behalf and make more demands of the school.

Conclusion
This is the backdrop to parental involvement at Brightside and Acre Lane; it is not the complete picture. It represents the conditions in which parents' involvement may or may not be pursued or enacted. As will be seen later, behind this seemingly positive picture lie disagreements, criticisms and tensions.

The two schools are quite similar in their organisation and management, and in particular in their strategies for relating to parents. Communication strategies, reporting strategies and disciplinary strategies are almost the same. A further similarity is of course in the various imperatives imposed upon schools by the competitive market: both schools, for example, were driven by the need to recruit students and retain them and the need at least to maintain, and in the case of Acre

Lane to improve, their examination successes and their standing in the league tables; related to this, both schools recognised the need for the support of parents.

Here, however the similarities end, since the kinds of support given by the majority of parents in the two schools differed. At Brightside the parents were an integral part of the school, characterised by their dominance on the governing body. But at Acre Lane parents remained much more outsiders. Lareau (1989) found in her research at a small number of primary schools in the USA that relations between working-class parents and the school were characterised by 'separation' or 'dissonance', whilst middle-class parents developed relationships characterised by 'interconnectedness' between family life and that of school (p.8). She describes how middle-class parents view education as a shared responsibility between themselves and the teachers, and might be very critical at times of their children's school experience and of the teachers themselves, intervening if they see it as necessary to do so. Working-class parents on the other hand rarely intervened in their children's schooling, and saw the responsibility for education as that of the teachers. These findings correspond with my own. However, unlike Lareau's work my study is of parents of secondary-aged children, and although she found that the working-class parents helped their children little with their school work, or did so inconsistently, I found that working-class parents were very supportive of their children's education: they wanted them to do well and if they could help them with homework (although that was not always possible) or support them in any way, they generally endeavoured to do so. This has also been found in other studies, for example Connell *et al.* (1982) and Reay (1998). However, this support was rarely visible to the school and it was much less overt than that of the majority of middle-class parents.

What has been presented here is the case of two schools which have very similar parent-school policies and practices but quite different parental responses. However, we also have two broadly different groups of parents, whose perspectives and whose own experiences of education, whose personal, social and economic circumstances, and whose expectations of the school are all different. Nevertheless, the relationship of the school to the parent body resonates with the maxim 'we treat them all the same'. What we have learnt from anti-racist research is that this is in effect a discriminatory stance (Troyna and Vincent, 1994). There is an implication that in spite of being treated the same (and therefore 'fairly') the working-class parents still do not respond appropriately, from the school's perspective; that the parents are at fault rather than that the approach by the school is itself inappropriate. There is no recognition of difference and thus no valuing of difference. I am not talking here solely about cultural differences, although these are important, but there are structural constraints upon the parents' actions. For example, as will be seen, even though the same amounts of information were sent out to all parents in both of these schools, middle-class parents had much more information about education both generally and specifically than the working-class parents (see also Reay, 1998 on this).

A further issue raised at the start of the chapter was to do with institutional bias: whilst this will generally be determined by the teachers and the senior management of the school, given the changing importance of parents and school governors this is no longer entirely the case. At Brightside the predominant middle-class group of parents was powerful and placed both demands and expectations upon the school, which, it is suggested, affected the institutional bias in terms of teacher responsiveness to their needs. At Acre Lane the middle-class parents were in the minority but again usually found satisfaction from their interventions and in questioning the decisions and practice of teachers. They did, however, hold power in the context of the market and the recognition that the school needed them and their children (see Chapters 3 and 5).

In the chapters that follow I explore further the relationship between the parents and the schools; as part of this I look at the differences between the relationships of different social groups of parents, as well as the similarities, with a view to illuminating the problems and possibilities of 'partnership'. Also I look at the influences upon different parents' involvement and in so doing highlight an interrelation of factors which overwhelmingly for working-class parents but at times for middle class parents too, militates against a partnership with the school/teachers.

In the following chapter I will look at the parents' perspective on their own involvement: what they do and why they do it, and the teachers' views on this.

Chapter 3

Parental involvement: what is it?

Introduction

Whilst some research has demonstrated the value of parental support in relation to literacy and numeracy skills at primary level (see for example Merttens and Newland, 1996; Topping 1986,1996), little attention has been paid as to whether parental involvement is either useful, desirable or indeed viable at secondary level from the perspectives of parents, teachers and the students themselves (Crozier, 1999b). Parental involvement is presented as a unified concept but in fact typologies of parental involvement (Vincent, 1996), parental roles (Meighan and Siraj-Blatchford, 1997) and indeed the nature of partnership (Pugh, 1989) have all been identified, illustrating the diversity of its practice and interpretation. As already stated, these interpretations are also variously acceptable or unacceptable to the key actors, depending upon their different constituencies and different situations (Crozier, 1999b).

The purpose of this chapter is to depict the nature of parental involvement as enacted and experienced by the parents and perceived by the teachers in the two study schools. It will be shown that by their actions, parents have divergent views of their involvement which do not always, and in some cases rarely, match with the expectations of the teachers. The chapter is not intended to outline all the different facets and manifestations of parental involvement but rather demonstrates the different ways that middle-class and working-class parents relate to their children's school. It will be shown that middle-class parents are much more visible than working-class parents in their relationships with the school, which presents its own challenges for the teachers. The invisibility of working-class parents is frequently interpreted as indifference (Beresford and Hardie, 1996). However, it will be shown that working-class parents are just as committed and supportive of their children's education as middle-class parents. The chapter also begins to raise the issue of difference: different practices, different ways of being and different values – not in the sense that working-class parents do not value education, but in the sense that they have different expectations of the home-school relationship; it will also be shown that the failure to appreciate difference leads to pathologisation of certain parents and the need for assimilation (Allen, 1999).

Expectations of parents by the schools and the teachers

Parental involvement has been imposed upon secondary schools from outside the profession. Perhaps because of this, secondary schools have been ill-prepared for the advent of the parents' new role. The two schools in this study said that they welcomed 'parental involvement'. Brightside included a statement in its prospectus which indicated its position on parental involvement, 'Working with parents in the best interests of the children,' which the head teacher asserted, sent out 'a very loud partnership model'. He also said, as already reported, that the governing body was dominated by parents, and on this basis he claimed, 'So yes, I think there is an overall policy of partnership.' But the parents were given little indication of what the school expected of them.

Acre Lane included the need to develop parent-school relationships in its five-year 'business plan and yearly school development plan' but there was no statement in the information to parents outlining what the expectations were. When asked, 'Does the school have any particular expectations of parents, of parental involvement?' the head of lower school at Acre Lane replied: 'Implicitly I think it does; I don't know that it declares it particularly.' The head of the upper school was equally vague: ' It's not as clear cut as that [specific school expectations of parents] ...there are references to, you know, keenness to have parental involvement and parental support.'

There were of course general expectations of parents, in terms of parents ensuring that the children arrive in school on time, wear school uniform, behave appropriately, and do their homework (Crozier, 1999a). Parents in both schools were expected to sign a homework diary, to comment on termly report cards or the annual progress report, and at Acre Lane to respond to the needs identified by spotlighting, as explained in Chapter 2. Such expectations were articulated by individual teachers in various ways:

> We would expect them to send their children to school on time, every day, in the correct uniform, with the correct equipment. We have a homework diary... it's like a personal organiser really ... and the parents sign that once a week. So we'd expect parents to monitor their children's homework and if they get stuck a lot of parents will want to help them with it. But obviously we never set homework that demanding, in case some children didn't have parents who could or would do it. So once a week they're supposed to check the diary as well. Every time there's a report, or a grade card, parents are expected to comment on it ... We would expect them just to be generally supportive of their child as they go through school and supportive of us in the efforts that we're making to help their children. (Head of year, lower school, Brightside)

> I suppose what I would like, is that parents encourage their children to do their homework, do their revision and hopefully provide them with a place where they can do their homework. I wouldn't expect them to get involved in the 'nitty gritty' although that would be nice if they did. I mean sometimes parents come and talk to me about extra help for their kids and I've always taken a line then, it never does harm if you feel you want to do that for your child. (Subject head, Acre Lane)

> ... things like bringing the child or getting the child to school, getting the pupil to school with pens and the right books and signing the homework diary; the low level things. And to be supported if there's any disciplinary action taken, I suppose I do expect that. It always comes as a shock to me that parents will, you know, defend the children and not let them do detention and all that sort of stuff... (Head of year 9 tutor, Brightside)

Nevertheless, the requirements to fulfil these expectations of involvement were not set out explicitly to parents. In fact the head of upper school at Acre Lane, anticipating perhaps what has now become a statutory requirement (as from September 1999, although not legally enforceable), said that he thought there was some merit in 'having some sort of contractual sort of statement which sets down what we the school will offer, what in return we expect the parents and the pupils themselves to offer ...'

Teachers' definitions of parental involvement appeared to see parents as a source of back-up to the teachers rather than the parents actively initiating anything themselves. The head of Brightside was particularly concerned about this aspect, even though the parents here were in fact very involved in the running of the school: 'You know it would be really counter-productive to put *too much* [my emphasis] energy into looking to see parents involved in the delivery of education as well as the monitoring.' The emphasis then is upon monitoring the children based upon the children's needs as identified and defined by the teachers. Lareau (1989) observed that the definition of 'partnership' 'implies a relationship between equals where power and control is evenly distributed' (p.35). Drawing on her research findings she goes on to say, 'Teachers did not... want to be equal with parents ...they wanted parents to defer to them and to their decisions in the classroom' (p.35).

The activities of a minority of parents, at both schools, in the wider sphere of the school, such as on the governing body, a Curriculum Policy Group, the Parent Teacher Association at Brightside (which organised information events as well as fund-raising) and participation in the Parents' Forum meetings at Acre Lane (which could in theory influence policy), could be seen, in contrast to Lareau's observations, to be evidence of the schools' attempts to develop the partnership beyond one of mere support. However, the reality of this, in my study also, was that very few parents were involved in this way at Acre Lane, whilst at Brightside the power of the parents posed a particular challenge for the school, in terms of managing this and balancing a 'useful' contribution against perceived 'interference'.

Additionally, the senior management in the two schools expressed the importance of parental involvement in terms of the educational market. Acre Lane, though the largest school in the area, was very conscious that as a result of parental 'choice' its numbers could be under threat; and furthermore the pupil intake was declining because of demographic trends. For the city as a whole, parental opt-out into neighbouring areas was a growing problem and one which the Local Education Authority had charged all secondary schools to address. Acre Lane also had an image problem; being located within a working-class area and having suffered poor examination results in the past it was intent upon improvement. Middle-class parents were few in number and were thus particularly valued; in the words of one member of the senior management team:

> We've got to recognise, in the harsh reality of the education world, that the parents of those quite few most able youngsters are quite important to us as a school because it gives us the results that we need to remain a successful school in the eyes of parents.

As well as having to respond to the change in parents' expectations of schools, and to some parents employing their new found 'rights', the senior management teams were beginning to recognise the need to bring parents 'on board' to ensure the success of the school and thus of the students. At Brightside this often entailed managing what at times amounted to the overenthusiasm of the parents, whilst at Acre Lane the senior management team was concerned with trying to facilitate a change in attitude. As the head of key stage 3 explained:

> There's a culture out there of wanting to get parents on board in terms of them getting involved in learning but there's also a culture change we want from them, to get them to realise that we mean business as far as learning's concerned as well.

Teachers are expressing here a unified view of a 'norm': the 'normal' way that they expect parents to behave (Foucault, 1977). When parents fail to meet this expectation, strategies need to be employed to ensure that this is brought about. The report cards, the parents' meetings, the spotlighting and target-setting are all devices for seeking normalisation. But at the same time they also serve to differentiate: to identify differences and to subject parents to scrutiny through the ongoing recording of the child's progress (Allen, 1999).

Parents' roles and responsibilities

When parents were asked directly about their roles and responsibilities in relation to their child's schooling, they tended to respond with similar answers to the teachers and each other. These included for example:

> It is largely a supportive one. I think it's about assisting them [the children] with getting information; it's about providing them with the equipment they need... (Mr Bristow, year 7 father, social class II, mother social class II, Brightside)

It's my role to make sure that they go out of the house in the morning clean and tidy, isn't it? And in the right frame of mind; if they go out thinking 'happy' then they're happy when they [get] to school. I mean however bad-tempered you feel in the morning, you don't show the kids. (Mrs Brookes, year 7 mother, social class III, father social class VII, Brightside)

Ensuring that their children were happy at school and that they were getting on 'well', as far as they perceived what 'getting on well' might be, were key concerns for parents. But in order to achieve this within the day-to-day interactions between parents and school, parental involvement was more diverse and more complex than their own definitions suggest. Parental involvement amounted to more than just making sure that the children had the right equipment and uniform and had done their homework. Parents are encouraged to play an active part in their children's learning; they are encouraged to buy the 'right' books and provide experiences to 'broaden horizons and excite imaginations' (Barber, 1996 p267). In doing such things they are traversing the boundary between home and school, they are stepping into the teachers' domain. Of course teachers want parents to provide interesting, imaginative and motivated children but as Lareau (1989) observed in her study 'teachers wanted to control ... the amount of inter-connectedness between home and school' (p.35). As has already been said, middle-class parents' relationships with the school were characterised by an interconnectedness with the school which was advantageous in the sense of being a positive relation, but which also gave rise to a source of tension. For working-class parents on the other hand, this was not the case; their dissonance with the school was, nevertheless, also a source of tension and led teachers to regard them somewhat disparagingly.

In the next two sections I want to show how parents sought to meet the needs of their children with regard to ensuring their happiness, well-being and progress at school. I have termed this aspect of involvement 'interventions' and I present the data illustrating it in terms of social class (as well as gender) in order to compare and contrast the different practices that middle-class and working-class parents employed, to meet their children's needs and fulfil their self-defined roles.

Middle-class parents' interventions

Middle-class parents said that they did not intervene if their children were doing well and were happy. They did nevertheless appear to require less prompting when they did do so; they were unhesitant about voicing an opinion or sharing a minor concern with the teacher. For example Mrs Pye (year 7 mother, social class III, father social class II, Acre Lane) explained that she wasn't really involved in any way at Acre Lane. She had a number of young children and so time was a factor in this. Also, even though she said she had kept abreast of educational matters (she had undertaken one year of a teacher-training course) she felt unqualified to intervene at this (secondary school) level. Nevertheless, she then went on to say:

> If there's anything that I feel isn't appropriate, then I would say but I'm not the professional... I'll leave it up to them, unless I actually feel it's impairing the children's work or wellbeing in anyway. Then I might get involved. I think possibly, maybe with Charles. Charles is a bit of a dreamer, his concentration is poor and I maybe said to the teacher: 'Look you'll have to put a bit more effort into making sure that he's understood what you've said or something like that, or speaking to him about certain aspects of things...'

Mrs Pye's statement is indicative of a self-confidence that middle-class parents had in talking with the teachers. In fact her intervention veers on an instruction to the teacher, telling her/him what s/he should do. Rather than 'I'm not the professional', she in fact places herself on at least an equal footing with the professionals, if not a superior one (see also Connell *et al.*, 1982 on this point).

Mr Hoyle (year 9 father, social class II, mother social class II, Acre Lane) also demonstrated this confidence and a sense of having the right to ensure his son's needs were met. He explained that he only intervened 'when they've [the children] got a problem'. He explained a number of incidents relating to his son's school experience. In one of these, 'he had a problem with a French teacher'.

> She wrote some comments on some homework which suggested he wasn't doing any work, that he wasn't trying. I felt, having talked to him... that it was more to do with the teacher. So I wrote saying that I felt the comments weren't very helpful and that I didn't accept them ...We had a meeting and thrashed it out...

Mr Hoyle went on to say,

> If I think things are wrong I won't let them lie. I will write...it's no good
> letting it sit and fester, you've got to bring it up and make your feelings
> known and they respond. You know they don't ignore you, things happen.
> I can't remember, there must be loads of letters I've written on different
> subjects. Even up to, you know, if I'm not happy I write to the head master.

Mr Hoyle was not an unhappy parent. He found the school very responsive but he made it his business to inform the school of his son's needs and more significantly to call the teachers to account.

At Brightside one parent coined the term 'giving a nudge or steer' when an issue came up (Crozier, 1997), which illustrated an attitude amongst parents that they had to make sure that teachers were kept 'on the right track', monitoring not just their children's work but also that of the teachers. Middle-class parents were clear about their equal standing with the teachers. Mr Bristow (year 7 father, social class II, mother social class II, Brightside) expressed it thus: 'It's not... a differential relationship because of our own background... [we are] professionals in our own right; so you know we do have a set of expectations about the standard that the school provides' (quoted in Crozier, 1997). This is further illustrated by an example of a parent who in response to the school taking action against a child who extorted money from her son, persuaded the head of year (who had contacted her) not to suspend the accused child. She explained:

> I talked to him and told him about the possibility that Scott might have
> offered the money because he knows the child and that it was a joke. And
> so he decided not to suspend the child which I actually, in a way, per-
> suaded him [not to do]. (Mrs Marchant, year 7 mother, social class II,
> father social class I, Brightside)

This is in marked contrast to those parents who preferred to maintain a low profile and leave such matters to the professionals. Unlike working-class parents, as will be seen, middle-class parents were also more inclined to intervene if the curriculum or teaching was not to their or their children's satisfaction. Subject choice was an issue which in particular gave rise to parental interventions. Mr and Mrs Banks (year 9 parents, mother social class III, father social class II, Acre Lane) for example, first spoke to and then wrote to the head teacher because their daughter had to do double science and was not therefore allowed to do double languages and double humanities which is what she wanted to do. The interchange between themselves and the head as recounted by Mrs Banks was as follows:

> We talked to the headmaster and first of all he said, 'We want all children to do double science, that's the way to go.' And we said, 'But we don't agree with you, not all children want to do that.' So anyway he said, 'If you write to me I'll look into it.' As I say, to his credit, he's changed it now to accommodate [seven or eight children].

Where the teaching was not thought to be adequate, middle-class parents were quite ready to call the teacher or the school to account. Mr Bristow (referred to above) recalled an occasion when he and his wife, who was a teacher and a deputy head, complained about their son's history teacher. He explained:

> [Paul] had a particular teacher at [Brightside]who was clearly incompetent. I mean sort of, never knowing their names; setting homeworks which were actually impossible, 'cos they were asked to find out about the Battle of Manchester in the Civil War when no such battle exists...So that was where we used parents' evenings; I mean having written to actually talk to, not only her, about what she was doing but also to talk to her head of department and the deputy head.

As a result of this intervention the school moved the teacher to another class.

Although not all middle-class parents were constantly clamouring at the door of the school, they were there, or on the telephone, when they felt this to be necessary. Whilst working-class parents have been similarly motivated, their response was much more restrained, the difference appearing to lie in the perception of what is 'necessary'. This perception is influenced by the middle-class parents' confidence, educational knowledge and experience; indeed, as Reay (1998) explains, by the parents' habitus and cultural capital. I will discuss this point and the influences upon parental involvement more fully in the next chapter.

Middle-class parents did not always get a satisfactory response, but they did in the majority of cases they recounted to us. Two examples where parents expressed dissatisfaction with the school response are outlined here. Mrs Rington (year 7 mother, social class III, father social class II, Brightside) explained that she was concerned about what she described as the repetitious work that her child had to do as a result of the school not streaming the class. She said that her child was 'ahead' at primary school and had already undertaken secondary-school-level work. She said that she went to the school to talk with the teachers, and described the response:

> I've been quite disappointed... I haven't been particularly satisfied with their response... I've had the response that I've been made to feel a bit pushy and that my own ideas are not necessarily right and I feel quite insulted by that actually. Whatever my ideas are, they're my ideas and I want [them] for my children.

Mrs Hoskins (year 11 mother, social class III, father social class II, Acre Lane) recounted her son's experience over a work-experience placement. She explained that the school had promised to arrange his work experience with an engineering firm. When they heard nothing, Mrs Hoskins telephoned the school to enquire and was told that the arrangements were in hand. Some time later they received a letter from the school reprimanding her son for not organising his placement. When Mrs Hoskins intervened again the head of year told her that it had nothing to do with him. She went on: 'I told him, 'I want you to look into it and tell me what happened.' To this day he's never done so. And we had to sort out [Joe's] work experience by ourselves...I was very upset.'

The research of Vincent et al. (2000) showed that middle-class parents found schools to be as inaccessible as did working-class parents. With a few exceptions such as those just described, this was not the case at either Brightside or Acre Lane. At Brightside there was a critical mass of middle-class parents who presented themselves as a powerful group. Many of them were professionals who held high-status jobs and in a number of cases they were either university lecturers or teachers. At Acre Lane, whilst middle-class parents were in the minority and tended to occupy service and managerial sector jobs, they nevertheless represented an important group for the school in that their children were perceived as high or potentially high achievers. High academic achievement was important for the school in the competitive market of a target-setting agenda.

Most of the actions of the parents were on an individual basis. However, at Brightside there were some examples of mini-collective action which again reaped rewards for the parents and their children. One incident again concerned option choice: a small group of parents protested about what was on offer and as a result the school accommodated the needs of five students. Another occasion was concerned with the school having introduced a lunch-time club for 'the most able' students. A group of parents were outraged by this and having let their feelings be known to the head teacher, the initiative was withdrawn.

These examples demonstrate power relations and 'struggles' between the parents and the school, and at times individual teachers. Whilst few parents would describe themselves as consumers in relation to their children's school, the nature of these interventions by middle-class parents could arguably be referred to as consumerist acts rather than as examples of partnership. In each of these incidents the parents were telling the teachers what they (the teachers) should be doing or what they (the parents) wanted, in order to protect their interests, or rather, those of their children. In most cases here, the parents seem to have had the upper hand but as I will now show this was not the case for working-class parents.

Working-class parents' interventions

In spite of the prevailing view that working-class parents are indifferent to or lacking in support for their children's education, working-class parents in this research study were very supportive of their children. Moreover, there was a frequently expressed commitment to working with the school, even though this did not usually mean in an overt way, as this interview with Mrs Dyer (year 7 mother, social class VII, father social class VI, Brightside) shows:

> *Interviewer:* As a parent, then, at the school, how do you see your role? What kind of things do you think you should do?
>
> *Mrs Dyer:* Basically working with the school to bring our children up into decent adults, basically. I mean schools set out guidelines, rules etc. for school and home and we try to work on that really.

She could, in other words, be talking about 'partnership' or at least one version of 'partnership'; indeed as she said later on in the interview, 'It's our responsibility which to me is working with the school.' Many parents had accepted the rhetoric of 'partnership' but different parents and teachers had different interpretations of it. Using Mrs Dyer as an example again, whilst she saw her role as working with the school this manifested itself in what was perceived by teachers, as a passive role – indeed, as non-involvement; she goes on to say: 'You know obviously if something happens at school, if it's important enough, they'll contact us.' However, as she also explains, 'I trust their judgement on these things. I don't really get involved a lot with the school ... I do trust them to sort of judge my children in that field [the academic] because they're the experts and I'm not basically.'

Mrs Milton (year 11 mother, social class VII, father social class V, Acre Lane) said a similar thing: 'I mean if I was worried I'd give the school a ring and ask if I could see the teacher, or them, as probably, if they were worried, I should imagine they would – um write and let us know.' Trust in the teacher by working-class parents was a dominant theme underpinning their relationship with the school. It was particularly significant in that working-class parents relied on the teacher to inform them of their children's progress and alert them to any problems which might need their support or action. In most cases parents believed their children to be 'doing well' and so there was no need, as far as they could see, to intervene in any way – as for example with Mrs Laurel (year 7 mother, social class III, father social class V, Acre Lane): 'They've all done well, so when the report comes through it's all good reports. So I'm not that concerned because I can see they're getting on well.'

The child's happiness was just as much a concern for working-class parents as for the middle-class parents discussed above and was thus a key factor in prompting a parent's intervention. As Mrs Price (year 7 mother, social class unwaged, father social class IV, Acre Lane) explained, 'If there was something worrying her [her daughter] I'd go in and discuss it with the teacher.' And as Mrs Dyer (see above) said, 'If the children come home and say, 'We're being bullied', or something, then we contact the school, you know.' Although working-class parents tended to intervene in academic matters less than middle-class if the child was unhappy then the parent would act. Mrs McClelland (year 9 mother, social class IV, father social class IV, at Acre Lane), for example, contacted the school when her son decided that he did not want to do dance as one of his options. The teacher refused to allow her son to give it up and when he insisted that he wasn't going to do it he was sent out of the class. Mrs McClelland explained: 'I phoned up the school and said, 'This isn't right, you're not tackling the problem.' And now he's been moved.'

Mrs Horn (year 7 mother, social class unwaged homeworker, father social class IV, Acre Lane) raised a question about an academic matter with a teacher only when her daughter asked her to do so, when she went to a parents' evening. Mrs Horn explained: '...my youngest does science and is totally bored with the subject, because they're just work-ing from books all the time ...' When she raised this with the teacher she was told, 'That's the way it's done.' Mrs Horn was resigned to this res-ponse feeling that she should trust the teacher's judgement, even though she also harboured, a view that this teacher lacked a certain amount of imagination:

> Now if I wanted to pursue it higher I would ...but what do you do? If she's a good teacher she's told me the truth and 'That's the way it's done.' Maybe another teacher who had a bit more imagination might do it a different way, I don't know. So to a certain extent you've got to go along with it.

Again this parent indicates that to take the matter further the issue would have had to have been more 'serious': '...if I was really, really concerned, I would go up and say so; I wouldn't have any qualms about doing that.'

For other parents too, there had to be a very strong reason to go to the school to intervene. As Mrs Bailey (year 11 mother, social class III, lone parent, Acre Lane) explained:

> I mean, if I had any problems, as I say, if I had any serious problems where he's not understood any of his work, if he can't make head nor tail of it [I'd go] up to the school with him. ...As I say the only time I really needed to get involved with the school was when Joe got beaten up.

Even a parent who did have a concern or wasn't entirely happy may decide not to contact the school, as in the case of Mrs Gale (year 7 mother, social class III, father social class V, Acre Lane):

> *Mrs Gale:* They've got study planners that they've all been given and in there you write your comments...and they're supposed to write back to you if there's little comments that they want to say and there's nothing ever written in there. One time I wrote that 'I wondered whether Jenny was completing all her homework in class because she didn't seem to be getting a lot of homework. Is she not set any?' And I had nothing back from that at all.
>
> *Interviewer:* Have you ever phoned up the school to talk to the tutor or anybody?
>
> *Mrs Gale:* No, no.
>
> *Interviewer:* Have you thought about it?
>
> *Mrs Gale:* Not about homework. I think I'd wait and – until I see him face to face. I'd only phone up if I thought there was a problem with Jenny that something was happening at school and she wasn't happy or being bullied or something.

Some parents saw going up to the school or telephoning about home-work and academically related matters as interfering in their children's lives and felt strongly that they didn't want to do this; as Mrs Stewart (year 7 mother, social class VII, father social class VII, Brightside) explained, even though she was concerned that her daughter's work was not being marked regularly, she did not intervene because:

> I don't like fussing. I'm not one of those that gets onto the school every two minutes because I think the kids have got to find their feet. Well you can't be with them all the time; they've got to establish themselves as their own people haven't they?

Not wanting to 'fuss' or be seen as a 'pushy parent' was a particular concern of working-class mothers (see also Reay, 1998). Indeed they were often quite critical of those who were ' always going up' to the school, and shared with some teachers, as will be seen later, the view that these parents were taking up teachers' valuable and scarce time: time which could be spent on their own children. As Evans and Vincent (1995) say, the 'discourse of consumerism is clearly a strongly individualistic one...consumers employ their particular resources in an effort to secure the type of provision or product which they have chosen' (pp.7-8). Individual parents' actions can serve to discriminate against other parents. Working-class parents as will be seen may have had few resources to deploy in this way. They nevertheless were not oblivious to the consequences for them and their children of other parents' actions.

There was a view amongst these working-class parents that the 'pushy' parents and those who were always involved in these high profile activities tended to benefit from them. Mrs Dyer (year 7, social class VII, father social class father VI, Brightside) explained it thus, although not particularly talking about Brightside:

> ...as they've gone up through the different schools, ... if a child has a mother or father that's a parent governor, or has anything to do with the school at all, then the children get all the prizes at the end of term...

> It's happened time and time again at the end of term you always know who is going to get the prizes...You can just see the parents there in the front seats or at the school musicals; the parents who help in the school get reserved seats. And I just don't think its fair at all.

Parents whose children had special educational needs and were statemented, tended to have more contact with individual teachers. One mother contrasted the contact she had with the school for her two children, the daughter having been statemented:

> We've had such close contact with [Acre Lane] with [Jackie] ... I don't know [Tom's] teacher. I've never had any need to know them but with [Jackie] we've had to build up that relationship to ensure that she actually achieves. (Mrs Lang, year 7 mother, social class III, father social class V, Acre Lane)

As a result of this she had got to know the teachers and saw this as being important in enabling them to get what their daughter needed.

Mrs Land, (year 9 mother, social class III, father social class VI, Brightside), whose child also had special educational needs, explained the intervention she took when she realised that her child needed extra support:

[Susie's] got problems, she's in the language unit...they didn't find this out until [pause] anyway they said, 'No, it was behaviour'. Anyway they had a special needs teacher come and they found that [Susie] had a really serious problem and then it was push, push, push to get her in there [Brightside].

And also regarding the junior school Mrs Land explained: 'I mean I did pester; I was a pain.'

Working-class parents do therefore intervene when they see the need for it. According to the account presented here their perception of this need would seem to be different from that of middle-class parents. Working class parents are more willing to defer to the teachers' judgements.

Discussion

The perceptions, knowledge and contact with the school displayed by middle-class parents are described by Atkin and Bastiani (1988a) as 'the development of familiarity'. Through this development, they say, parents' sense of parenting becomes more closely aligned to teaching, parents develop a more positive view of school life and they become more proactive in developing strategies to tackle perceived difficulties that affect their children (p.59). This is a very similar view to Lareau's (1989) analysis of the consonance middle-class parents have with the school. As she showed in her study, whilst working-class parents tend to be more distant and marginalised from the school (as shown here too), middle-class parents have a more comfortable relationship, or indeed a 'fit', with the school, the teachers and the social and organisational milieu. Middle-class parents thus operate on a more equal footing with the teachers and feel able to engage teachers in a discussion about their children's needs. As Connell *et al.* (1982) remind us, 'the relation between teachers and parents has to be understood as a class relation' (p.128). In my study this has most significance for working-class parents, who are positioned in a less authoritative position in relation to teachers than are middle-class parents (*ibid.*).

There are therefore consequences for the parents according to how they are regarded by the teachers. Beresford and Hardie (1996) suggest that involvement by parents can influence teachers' perceptions of parents, and indirectly of their children, serving to raise their esteem, at least in the sense that the parents are 'on the teachers' side'. Johnson and Ransom (1988) have argued too that 'teachers evaluate parental support in the secondary school by the extent to which they visit the school.' Working-class parents who visit much less often than middle class parents are thus frequently regarded as either unsupportive or indifferent.

As well as the kind of interventions described above, a minority of mainly middle-class parents were involved in a variety of other types of activity, such as various committee-type work (referred to in chapter 2), transporting children to and from sports fixtures, supporting school concerts in various practical ways and fund-raising; or being selectively invited into school to speak on a topic about which they had expertise. All of this added to their visibility.

However, there are areas of involvement by middle-class parents as well as working-class parents which tend to be invisible. In spite of government rhetoric about parents being the child's 'first and enduring teachers' (DfEE, 1997a), the educational role that parents play in the home tends to be ignored or discounted. This is despite the boundary between home and school, as discussed in Chapter 1, becoming increasingly blurred.

Parents at home

Walkerdine and Lucey (1989) point out that there can be no distinctions between different kinds of housework or rather domestic labour: between shopping cooking, cleaning, mothering. As they say: '... we make no distinctions between what counts as housework and what counts as mothering, the 'work' of being a mother' (p.68). For parents, and particularly mothers, supporting their children has no boundaries and yet this 'emotional work' (Edwards and Alldred, 1999; Reay, 1998) is rarely acknowledged.

Whilst there is an implicit expectation that this 'work' goes on at home, there is not only an absence of recognition of its existence but also a dismissal of its relevance in that it does not accord with 'school-work'. We did not focus our data collection on this 'home-work' but its significance for this study lies in the lack of recognition schools give to the wider contribution parents make to their children's education and their failure to take adequate account of parents' knowledge of their own children.

Parents indicated that they were rarely, if at all, consulted about their children just as Maclure and Walker (1999) observed in their study of parents' evenings in secondary schools. Although they are often referred to paradoxically as 'consultations', there was little consultation in the sense of asking the parents for information about the child. Moreover, as Maclure and Walker report, 'Parents' attempts to offer unsolicited personal knowledge of the student (for example, home circumstances, emotional problems) were frequently overlooked or given minimal acknowledgement by the teacher' (p.8).

When Mrs Robson (year 9 mother, social class III, father social class VI, Brightside), for example, was asked, 'Do the teachers consult you, ask your opinions and views about your daughter?', she replied:

> No not really, does it? [turns to her husband] ...No they're usually telling you; we don't usually tell them. They don't ask. Only like the time John was being bullied she asked how he was feeling. But I don't think we've been asked for anything to do with their work.'
>
> *Mr Robson:* [Nor] how the school is run, anything like that, or how they teach the children, no.'
>
> *Mrs Robson:* They've never asked our opinions about our child; they've given their opinions.

Parents' 'home-school work' in relation to their children took on a variety of forms, from the monitoring so desired by the school, to helping with homework, providing support generally and providing equipment:

> Well I ask them everyday... what they have learnt in the day. If they turn round and say, 'I've learnt nothing', Well I say, 'well what have you been doing all day?!' It is very important to me for them to get an education. (Mrs Brookes, year 7 mother, social class III; father social class VII, Brightside)
>
> Because I have a child with special needs and he must have a textbook of his own, we say we'll supply one. We've done an awful lot of supplying resources and fortunately we've been able to. We're both [she and her

husband] stuck with pens on paper or fingers on keyboards, so we provide positive role models I guess. It's very easy to think you've got to do homework in a house like this. If you only had one room it would be incredibly difficult. (Mrs Higgins year 11 mother, social class II, father social class I, Brightside)

Well I wouldn't say I go through their homework every night because that would be a lie – I show interest. I think that's the most important thing. (Mrs Horn, year 7 mother, social class unwaged homeworker, father social class IV, Acre Lane)

Mrs Higgins also referred to occasional midnight shopping sprees for materials for school the next day. Again, as Mrs Higgins implies, middle-class parents are in a better position to do such things and to offer an example in line with the values of the school.

Some (middle-class) parents actively attempt to structure and develop their children's education, attempting to build on the school experience or seeking to ensure that the school experience builds on the home experience (Lareau, 1989). An example of this is clearly expressed by Mr Lennox (year 11 father, social class II, mother social class II, Brightside):

What we're pushing for all the time is for our children to fulfil their potential... With the younger one we're looking for him to be pushed all the time, with the older one we're looking for the teachers to minimise his work because he tends to try to do too much. You're just trying to get feedback from the teachers so that you can reinforce what's going on in the school, what you're trying to do at home.

Conclusion

It has not been my intention here to document every aspect of parents' involvement in the two secondary schools but rather to demonstrate the different types of involvement of middle-class and working-class parents. Middle-class parents have been seen as more visible and overtly interventionist, whilst-working class parents appear to be passive in educational matters, only making themselves visible at parents' evenings. This behaviour is interpreted by teachers as indifference and lack of support. I have shown through the parents' own voices that this is not the case; that whilst working-class are reliant upon teachers' judgements and place their trust in them, they are supportive and watchful of their children's progress. As Meighan and Siraj-Blatchford (1997) have said the 'good' parent does not need to be in agreement with the school but only to give the impression that they are and that they are fulfilling the school's criteria for a 'good parent'. They go on to say that middle-class parents may have more skill, not only in intervening on their child's behalf, but also in impression management with the teachers. Being seen to be involved, and being able to be interventionist is influenced by a collection of interrelating factors, experiences, knowledge and perspectives. It is to an exploration of these influences that I now turn.

Chapter 4

Layers of influence upon parental involvement

In this chapter I look at some of the many influences, or rather layers of influence, upon parental involvement with the school, in terms of intervening on their child's behalf, and in wider activities (outlined earlier) such as attending meetings, fund-raising or going to school concerts. These influences are layered discordantly rather like geological plates, since they can shift about and impact at different times or simultaneously.

Being involved in one's child's school and education in general, in whatever way and at whatever level, requires time, energy and commitment; material resources are an advantage too. Parents have these things to varying degrees; these factors and their impact upon the school relationship will be discussed at the end of the chapter in the section *Time factors and other commitments and concerns*. As well as these particular conditions for involvement, there are other influences which interweave and impact upon each other. These can be divided into three broad categories:

(i) the strategies the school employs to relate to parents and to keep them informed in order that they can feel a part, of their child's education; these will be discussed in *School-parent communication and Marginalisation – visible and invisible boundaries*

(ii) prior knowledge and experience, or what Bourdieu and Passeron (1977) termed cultural capital, and Bourdieu (1984) termed habitus which enable parents to utilise information from, and their relationship with, the school or else to compensate in various ways for what is lacking; these will be addressed in *Education knowledge* and *Networking – social capital accumulation*

(iii) the impact of both these sets of influences on parents, which will be discussed in the section *Teacher knows best*.

As will be apparent from the analysis already presented, social class and gender are overarching influences which for example have impacted upon parents' own educational experiences and the development of social and cultural capital, as well as on time and material resources. Social class and gender will thus be discussed in relation to the various layers of influence.

School-parent communication

Although it seems obvious that the wishes of the child about parental involvement in her/his schooling would be an influence upon parents, little consideration has been given to this either by policy-makers or by researchers (see Edwards and David, 1997, Edwards and Alldred, 1998 for exceptions to this). Frequently, parents said in their interview responses that they would help their children more if the children would allow them to. Some parents also took the view that their children should take responsibility for their own learning. The views of school students will be discussed in detail in Chapter 6.

However, as well as the students' desires regarding their parents' involvement, the performance and progress of the child and how the parent perceived this also influenced whether or not the parent felt the need to contact the school or take any action. As argued in Chapter 3, a key issue here is in the parents' perception of when it is appropriate to contact the school; as was shown, some parents were more zealous or demanding in this respect than others. Some parents may have been too reticent, or too reliant on the school's judgement. Prior experience, educational knowledge and self-confidence will have influenced the parents' perceptions and judgements but so too will the amount of information and the implicit or explicit encouragement on the part of the school.

Some parents were clearly unsure about how well their children were progressing. Whilst they may have been doing well, it was not always explained what 'well' meant or that such a judgement in itself was relative. Some parents, for example, either had not had explained to them the subject-tiering[1] system for General Certificate of Secondary

Education (GCSE) and its implications or else had not understood the information given. One example of this was Mr Woodside (year 11 father, social class VI, mother unwaged homeworker, Acre Lane) whose daughter wanted to go on to become a nursery nurse but needed GCSE Maths at grade C to get onto the course of her choice at the local College of Further Education. In year 10 she had been put up a set against her wishes. The parents were not consulted. In her mock exam she only gained grade F. The parents did not know which tier she had been entered for and the student and the parents were left feeling anxious about her future.

As reported in Chapter 2, parents in both schools and across social classes complained that they did not get enough information about their children's progress or what they did in school, or about how they could help with school work. This was recounted in the two questionnaires that were sent out to the parents as well as in interviews. This need was acknowledged by the head of Brightside, who identified with a similar problem of communication he had had with his daughter's primary school. As a result of this he said he was committed to looking into how they might improve such information for parents.

Other studies, such as Goacher and Reid (1985) and Jowett and Baginsky's (1991) Scottish study, have also reported that parents need more guidance on how they can help their children better. More recently Clarke and Power (1998), in their study of school reports to parents and parents' evenings, also showed that parents were dissatisfied with the information they received about their children's progress. This is in spite of the statutory reporting requirements for schools (see DfEE, 1997b and QCA/DfEE, 1997) and as Clarke and Power (1998) also found, the majority of schools (183 schools in their sample) 'reported to parents more frequently than legally required' (p.5).

Parents did report that they received an abundance of information especially at Brightside (details were given in Chapter 2). Although some admitted that they did not always read it, or perhaps not carefully enough, some also said that the information was not always clear and that they didn't always understand it. Sometimes too much information proved overwhelming, as Mrs Wilson (year 9 mother, social class III, father social class VI, Brightside) explained, when asked if they had received the school governors' annual report:

I can't remember whether we received it or not because you know we see so many letters. I really can't honestly say. I mean we most probably did but I'm not that aware of it ...As I say I'm not very clued up because I don't attend them [meetings]. I mean I should really but as I say I find them very difficult, a lot is very over the top.

The senior management teams of both schools emphasised the importance of keeping parents informed about what was going on in the school. A subject head at Brightside explained:

the more parents understand [then] our jobs are much better, you know, much easier ... If you ever get a parent interested, or phoning up or concerned, as long as you can meet them, as long as you can lay everything on the table and say 'This is what is going on' you rarely have problems.

This subject head was referring specifically to informing parents about the nature of the subject and the expectations regarding that discipline. Whilst this information would no doubt be useful for parents, it did not illuminate the educational progress of their own children. Nor did it necessarily give them guidance with respect to supporting their children's learning. Moreover, some subject departments were better than others in providing information.

As will be seen later, many teachers display an ambiguous position over parental help; on the one hand they are critical when parents appear to be unsupportive but on the other they are quick to condemn the so-called 'pushy parent' (McCormick, 1982). As McCormick commented, in relation to the primary phase of schooling: 'Reading stories with your child is applauded; buying your own copy of the school's reading scheme is definitely not' (p.313). This view prevailed to differing degrees amongst teachers and was largely dependent upon the nature of the subject. English departments tended to be keen to inform parents and involve them in certain types of project work such as 'biography', whilst mathematics departments felt that parental involvement could lead to confusion for the child.

Another problem seems to be the means by which information is sent home: usually via the student, who may forget to pass it on or lose it, and who may not want her/his parent to receive it anyway. Some teachers indicated a certain weariness about informing parents, as in the response of this subject head (Acre Lane):

> You sometimes get in Year 11 parents' evening, a parent will come up and [question] the predicted grade: 'I didn't know my kid was only able to get a maximum grade D in this set'. And I'm able to say, 'Well there's the letter that was sent home explaining this', so it is just to cover ourselves.

The problem was not a lack of information *per se,* but rather the type of information. Where information was given about the student's academic progress, such as at parents' evening, it was often vague and un-informative; this was also borne out by Maclure and Walker's research (1999). Mr Rigg (year 9 father, social class II, mother social class III, Brightside), for example, explained:

> Sometimes the comments are surprisingly bland, you might say. You feel... that you're being given the answers that you might like to hear... You want to hear where he's failing not where he's doing so well, and where we could help..

Mrs Dorn (years 7 and 11 mother, social class VII, father social class IV, Brightside), when asked about the school keeping her informed about her younger son's progress, replied:

> I don't feel I have [been kept informed], especially as he needs to be kept an eye on. And he needs extra support from home; no I don't think that's the case.
>
> *Interviewer:* So, when you've gone to parents' evening have you felt better informed?
>
> *Mrs Dorn:* Very vague. I've been amazed; it's been very vague. I mean I'm not getting complaints about him but I'm not getting anything... I know they've got facilities there which is great and he goes out for that special tutoring which is lovely, what I wanted, but the [gap] between them and us is wide.

Mrs Stanley (year 11 mother, social class III, father social class VII, Acre Lane) sometimes wondered if the teachers remembered who each individual child was: 'It's hard for them to remember seeing so many different people.' And with respect to the student's report she felt that the comment was more of a 'general thing'.

Mrs Stanley said she only knew about what her children did in school by going through their books. Some parents also remarked that teachers sometimes put a positive gloss on how the children were getting on because to do anything other than that would reflect badly on them.

As reported in the previous chapter the contact was closer with parents whose children had special educational needs. Another exception to this poor communication between teachers and parents was where parents had children who had been statemented (see also, for example, Vincent, 1996; Wolfendale, 1992). In these cases the children spent some time in a special unit in the school and as part of the statutory requirements there had to be contact between the school and the parents. As Mrs Gale (year 7 mother, social class III, father social class V, Acre Lane) observed:

> If your child is just plodding along and getting the right marks and things, they tend not to get in touch with you. I think if your child's an under-achiever they'll keep you more informed. If they're average you don't get a lot of input.

According to Lareau (1989) a lack of information about academic matters is related to an absence of particular social networks and social capital, this will be discussed later. One thing that is again indicated here is that working-class parents tend to wait to be informed by the school rather than to initiate contact with the school as the middle-class parents are inclined to do.

Educational knowledge

Although both middle-class and working-class parents experience poor communications from the school about the specific detail regarding their children, middle-class parents, because of their educational know-ledge (Crozier, 1997) and cultural capital (Bourdieu and Passeron, 1977) are better equipped than working-class parents to seek out and gain access to the information they want. Working-class parents, whilst desiring this information, appear more resigned to not having access to it and to relying on and trusting the teacher. In this section I will discuss this issue together with the nature of educational knowledge, and how such knowledge helps to advantage middle-class parents.

With the amount of media exposure that education has had on television and in the press, together with the publicity campaigns launched by the

DfEE, most parents have some knowledge of the various changes to the education system. However, class differences showed themselves in the extent that different groups of parents understood the various changes and in the way they articulated their understanding of educational issues. Middle-class parents were keen to talk in the interviews about a range of educational matters and issues such as those relating to OFSTED, league tables, post-16 education and gender issues, as well as the National Curriculum and assessment, thus demonstrating their educational knowledge and understanding. With regard, for example, to choosing a school Ms Douglas (year 11 mother, social class II, social class father II, separated, Brightside) demonstrated that her thinking was not crudely based on league tables but that she was equally if not more concerned about the ethos of the school:

> I don't look for exam results. I don't look for that sort of thing. I mean I'm interested but that's not the primary thing. I look first at the head and if I like the head that's a good beginning and then if I generally get the feeling that the basic facilities are sound that's what will make me decide on the school. Because if the head's good the rest is going to follow it seems to me and its certainly proved to be so. I feel these ideas of comparing results, exams, from one school to another is so misleading; it's okay in its way but it's not sufficient. It doesn't give you an idea at all of what the place is all about...

These parents' expectations of the school are frequently elaborated in terms of educating the whole child rather than just the academic side; as Ms Douglas also said:

> Well apart from providing as good an education as that child is capable of absorbing... it's the social element as well; taking for granted that she's going to get a reasonable education academically, the social aspect is incredibly important to me...

In talking about the National Curriculum, Ms Skinner (year 7 mother, social class II, father social class II, Brightside), for example, responded thus:

> I know masses of things are missed out of the National Curriculum. As far as I'm concerned there's lots of things I would like my children to learn at school that aren't part of the curriculum... I think dance should be on the curriculum. I think music from a very early age. All children dance

before they become self-conscious and I think the arts could be used in a much wider sense rather than, 'Oh let's just do painting today' or 'Let's do singing today'. I think it could embrace the world in a much larger sense in terms of humanities and mathematics, all kinds of things, measuring the rhythm you know, seasons, patterns.

The point being demonstrated here is the nature of middle-class parents' educational knowledge and understanding and in particular that they think broadly about the content of education and the experience they want for their children.

Although working-class parents knew about the National Curriculum they tended to have less desire to discuss it, at least in the interview situation; for example Mrs Foster (year 11 mother, unwaged homeworker, father social class VII, Brightside) was asked if she knew about the National Curriculum:

Mrs Foster: Oh there's certain subjects that they have to do, oh yeah.

Interviewer: How do you know about that?

Mrs Foster: That's obvious, it's been so widely publicised.

Interviewer: Through the media?

Mrs Foster: Oh yeah, and well, the schools as well. They send stuff home saying '[Jimmy] has to do this and he can't do that', all sorts of stuff.

Interviewer: Do you know about the assessments?

Mrs Foster: Yeah, the 1,2,3 bit, cos [Joey] [her youngest junior-aged child] has that. I don't think they do so much of that with the older kids but with [Joey] yeah.

Other working-class parents often said they didn't always understand the new developments; they found them complicated and unlike the system they had experienced at school.

Mrs Mornington (year 9 mother, unwaged homeworker, father social class V, Acre Lane)

It's changed so much! It's changed from last year, two years ago it changed again. I mean I'm confused. You go up and you listen to what they're doing in technology and all this lot [the National Curriculum]. Three systems of technology and you think, 'Oh yes'. Now it's gone...that's it, it's all gone.

> You know I'm confused, so I really do not know at the moment what is standard.

Mrs Crook (year 11 mother, social class III, father social class IV, Brightside), when asked if she had been told about the GCSE tiering and other such details, replied:

> I find it very confusing actually...it's when they bring all these, what do you call them nowadays, National Curriculum isn't it? I find that all very confusing.
>
> *Interviewer:* Have you had any information [about the National Curriculum]?
>
> *Mrs Crook:* I suppose we have but perhaps I've not grasped it properly. Sometimes it may not be written in a way you can understand basically...

Clarke and Power (1998) also remarked that 'For some parents, notably working-class parents and those with little or no English, school remains 'another country' with its inscrutable professional discourse' (p.51). Where a subject was technical, unless a parent had that particular expertise then the further the child progressed through the secondary school the less likely it was that the parent could help. However, the nature of the parents' own general education determined whether or not s/he could help in general ways such as with the process of writing an essay or discussing a literary text. Parents tended to say that they always tried to help, but as Mr Woodside (year 11 father, social class VII, mother social class unwaged homeworker, Acre Lane) said, when his daughter was studying *A Midsummer's Night's Dream* and found it too difficult, he was helpless himself to support her.

It would be incorrect to suggest that working-class parents did not have a view on their children's education or what they wanted from school for their children. The extent to which they articulated this varied, whilst most of the middle-class parents interviewed held forth about their children's academic ability, progress and educational experience. Working-class parents were very clear and precise that they wanted their children to be happy and to do as well as they were capable of doing. As Mrs Parker (year 11 mother, social class III father social class VI, Acre Lane) put it:

> We expect that from the day they go in to the day they come out that they're going to be made ready. We'll we do our bit; I expect them [the school] to do their bit... From what I can get from the school I think the school [is doing their bit]. The proof of the pudding is when they eventually leave.

Some working-class parents were more analytical about the educational experience. Ms Tasker (year 9 mother, social class III, lone parent, Acre Lane) felt strongly that her son's needs were not being met:

> The government has screwed up in education. The way I look at it is like every other country, they can speak four or five languages at the age of like 15 and my son can only speak English, maybe a bit of French, maybe a bit of German. But what's happening with the school education is that there's not enough time to be spent on education. If you work it out they have more days off of school [than when they're actually in school]... When they're actually in school they're maybe at seven or eight lessons a day which I don't think is very valuable because you're changing over different lessons all the time. There's nothing really going in and the timing is like you get three breaks...you know the concentration isn't going into the children, they're not getting enough concentration so when it comes to exam marks, it's only the upper class what are seeming to get to that grade because they've got the money to do it; because they've got the schooling, the background to concentrate on their children ...When you're well off you can turn around and say 'Have the teacher here tonight'. Or 'You can go to the music class tonight'. Or 'You can go to English', or there's Maths or whatever. But when you're ... like working class, mm, you have to go along with the school and education of today.

Middle-class parents talk about the school and education with confidence and authority and, as has been seen, they are confident about questioning the teacher or entering a dialogue on an equal footing:

> In other ways we regard the school as competent, you know as competent professionals and they will go on and deliver the job. We go there and convey our anxieties about [Paul's] presentation or perhaps his spelling and ask them to deal with that. We will take up particular issues if there are issues that are troubling our children. [Felicity] at the moment has got an RE teacher she finds is not presenting the curriculum in a way it's supposed to be presented, and he's very much wanting to convert them all to Christianity. (Mr Bristow, years 7 and 9 father, social class II, mother social class II, Brightside)

Similarly, when Acre Lane notified parents that the school rather than the students or parents, would be making the decisions about option choices, Mrs Falmer (year 11 mother, social class II, father social class I, Acre Lane) questioned this:

> I was strongly opposed, ... so I had words with him [the head], 'You know this doesn't seem fair and the whole point is we discuss it along with them [the option choices with the teachers and children] ...as to what their future was going to be and what they wanted to do and what they were interested in and what they were capable of doing and that was the whole point of having these options that we could all choose together.' And he said, 'Well you can write in and ask for changes to be made.' So I wrote in ... so that's what we did and so she's doing what she wanted.

It is not that working-class parents do not have educational knowledge and understanding but rather that middle-class parents have the same or similar knowledge to the teachers and they articulate this knowledge in the same language; they tend to occupy the same educational discourses. In discussing cultural capital, of which I suggest educational knowledge is here an aspect, Gewirtz *et al.* (1995) describe working-class parents as not having it 'in the right currency'. Ms Tasker has an analysis of her son's educational experience, one which teachers may agree with but which would have little or no resonance in relation to her son's schooling. She has a view of the bigger picture but not of the specifics. Her views are in some way disconnected.

The language issue is important here too. Labov (1969) for example in writing about the learning experiences of children and young people, demonstrated through his research the value judgements made of young people's language. Where the person did not use a standard form of language they were deemed to be inadequate and inferior, irrespective of the evidence. Such cultural mismatches between teachers and parents create barriers which according to Jacob and Jordan (1993) cause working-class parents to opt out.

Those parents who had educational knowledge had furthered their own education and were 'educationally confident'. What they did not know themselves they were able to find out either through appropriate channels of communication or someone who did know. Most of these parents tended to be the middle-class parents. Few working-class parents had any qualifications other than some CSEs or low-level vocational qualifications. Many of the mothers either did not go out to work and so had limited access to social capital (a point which will be discussed below), or had part-time unskilled jobs; the fathers were often self-employed in building-type or odd-job-related activities. Low paid, low status jobs add little to a person's social, cultural or in this case educational capital. These things also contribute to what Brown (1987) calls 'frames of reference', which in turn influences how the parents perceive themselves and consequently how they feel able to act. These experiences resonate with those of the working-class mothers in Reay's study (1998). Following Lareau (1989), Reay employs Bourdieu's concepts of habitus, field and cultural capital as explanatory tools 'for understanding the social processes within the home, in the classroom and between home and school' (p.32). In so doing, she seeks to demonstrate through her empirical work the impact of habitus and the embodiment of culture upon the mothers' involvement in schooling. As she says '...habitus emphasizes the importance of the social location people have come from as well as highlighting the social space they moved through, in order to reach their current position' (p.47).

The habitus of middle-class parents, together with their high status and relatively valuable cultural and social experiences, has armed them with the requisite self-confidence and knowledge to approach the school and access the information they require about their children, or to intervene if necessary. In their research on school governors and issues of active citizenship, Deem et al. (1995) discuss the importance of knowledge as an important resource for participation, especially in underpinning the self-confidence of those involved. As they say: 'This self-confidence may be related to a citizen's knowledge of the organizational arena in which they are participating. This includes knowledge of the particular, or local knowledge...' (p.53). They also found, together with Prestage (1994), that in predominantly working-class areas it is very difficult for school governing bodies to recruit and retain parent governors (p.53), suggesting a connection between the two.

The head of Brightside acknowledged the potential inequality of educational knowledge when, referring to the research report we produced for the school on the basis of the questionnaire to parents, he remarked:

> I was taken by the comment in your report which [said] that maybe we should do a bit more in actually showing parents how to help. To some parents it becomes instinctive because they're interested anyway but sometimes other parents actually need to be shown.

The different ways in which these two groups of parents talk about education is likely to have an effect upon their relationship with the teachers. The middle-class parents speak the same language as the teachers, and through this and the way they relate and respond to the school demonstrate what Lareau (1989) describes as their inter-connectedness. That is not to say that they always agree, but the issue here is much more about the conditions being right to enable parents to access information and acquire respect, in order to have their wishes met or at least to have their voice heard. Presenting themselves as articulate and educationally knowledgeable puts the balance of power between themselves and the teacher much more in their favour.

This was not the case for working-class parents. They were described by some teachers as 'less articulate' and the 'less articulate' were also said to be the 'less motivated'. This resonates with the discussion in the previous chapter regarding attendance at school events and the effect of this on teachers' perceptions of the parents.

In discussing higher education, Bourdieu *et al.* (1994) write about the distancing and misunderstandings between teachers and working-class students. If working-class parents feel, or are made to feel, as though they do not know enough about educational matters then it is likely that they will adopt a position, as Bourdieu et al term it, of 'resigned submission to being excluded'(p.9).

Teacher knows best

The overwhelming attitude of working-class parents at Acre Lane and at Brightside was to defer to the teachers' judgement, even though they may not always have been entirely happy with what was going on. This was endorsed by teachers at Acre Lane, as expressed here for example: 'I think parents by and large at [Acre Lane] are happy for us to get on with the job of education ...it's almost as if they say, 'Well that's your job' (head of year Acre Lane). David (1993b) points to Lareau (1989) and Scott (1990), who argue that working-class mothers do not perceive or recognise a value in their own involvement at their children's school. Likewise, in this study working-class mothers and fathers frequently deferred to the teachers' expertise and knowledge when asked if they would like more opportunities to have a say in their children's education.

> I do trust them to sort of judge my children in that field because they're the experts and I'm not basically. (Mrs Crook, year 11 mother, social class III, father social class VI, Brightside)

> *Mrs Robson:* ... surely the teachers should know what's right, what to teach the child? They should know more about it than I do.

> *Interviewer:* So you are quite happy to let the teachers get on with it?

> *Mrs Robson:* I don't think we've got the knowledge to do anything else. We're not that kind of academically aware, are we [turning to her husband]?

> *Mr Robson:* No. (year 9 parents, mother social class III, father social class IV, Brightside)

> I presume she's doing well. I presume if there was anything bad they would let me know, if she wasn't working. (Mrs Sweep, year 9 mother, social class III, father social class VI, Acre Lane)

> I don't think you should interfere. Unless, I think it's wrong practice. Then, yeh, if they're turning round and you know, if they're beating the hell out of [Josie] because she's turned up late ... I will interfere. If they are disciplining her because she's been rude...then that's right, you know I think they should do that. I think it's all relative isn't it? Do you know what I mean? I don't think I should interfere as such but on the other hand if it's wrong, then I will interfere. It depends on what you think is wrong. (Mrs Webb, year 9 mother, social class III, father social class VI, Acre Lane)

When Mrs Sweep was asked how she saw her role in relation to her daughter's schooling, she said:

> I think they ought to have a free hand. I think perhaps they [the school/the teachers] need [one] ... I don't think it helps if you keep going up nagging and carrying on. You know it just brings [Mary's] name into the forefront and perhaps it gets everybody needled.

Parents may feel more inclined to defer to the teachers because they feel the teachers have the expertise; but also there is very little choice if the parents don't have the information that the teachers have about their children. Mr Moss (year 9 father, social class IV, mother social class unwaged homeworker, Acre Lane) indicated this:

> Well obviously kids will be sort of totally different in a school environment than they will at home. I mean to a certain extent every parent likes to think they know their children but they don't actually know what they're like when they mix with other children and it's not until you get sort of the end of school or end of term's report home that you find out how well or how badly or whatever they're actually doing.

He went on:

> ...I must admit [with] the eldest, her report left a lot to be desired. The general sort of feeling was 'Not trying hard enough, could do better'. So she's on a warning for this term, 'Pull your socks up or else'.
>
> *Interviewer:* So you're supporting the school in what they're saying?
>
> *Mr Moss:* Oh yes, I think you have to because obviously you don't know, I mean once they leave home at 8 or 8.15 in the morning and don't get home till sort of 3.30 p.m. you don't know what they're up to and you rely on the teachers to tell you that.

Marginalisation, visible and invisible boundaries

Bourdieu *et al.* (1994) in their analysis of the lecturer-student relationship, discussed the significance of the organization of the lecture as part of this process of ensuring separation:

> Everything in the present organization of university teaching – from the physical form and the layout of the lecture theatre to the examinations regime and its criteria, from the assignments leading up to the exams to the organization of the curriculum – favours the reciprocal distancing of teacher and student. (p.10)

Likewise it can be argued that a similar set of boundaries is created in schools between teachers and parents. The parents' evening is a useful example of the tightly demarcated roles and expectations. In both schools, as is common practice elsewhere, parents have to make appointments with the teachers. Maclure and Walker (1999) have likened this to the medical consultation with the doctor. They found that the consultation began with a 'diagnosis' and teachers maintained control over the dialogue. They found, as was the case in this study, that there was little opportunity for parents to ask questions and even less to make an observation or put forward their own point of view. In this study the consultation lasted only ten minutes per teacher. Even parents who were confident and regarded themselves as being on at least an equal footing with the teachers said that they would not raise anything of significance with the teachers in this particular forum but would contact them later.

Many parents, irrespective of social class, reported that they found parents' evenings daunting, at times confusing and even chaotic. However, there were clear efforts by the senior management of both schools to manage parents' evenings. The appointment system and allocation of ten minutes per parent or family was one indication of this, and at Brightside staff had development sessions on managing parents' evenings and were given a list of do's and don'ts.

Middle-class parents described parents' evening as a public relations exercise either from the schools' perspective or indeed from their own. They felt that very little infomation was forthcoming and they tended to go in order to be seen to be doing 'the right thing' by the school or to show the children they were interested; to be supportive to the children and to put a face to the teachers.

> I go [to parents evening] and I hear the same things. I know what I'm going to hear ...I'd go and hear, 'Yes she's wonderful, she does this...' well I knew all that. I'm not sure whether it wasn't a waste of time sometimes, but I went for the children. I felt they should see me go and being involved. Also it gave the teachers an opportunity but I think if they had anything to really say it would be something we'd do one to one on another occasion. (Mrs Thomas, year 11 mother, social class I, lone parent, Brightside)

Working class parents also found that little information was forthcoming: Mrs Brown (year 11 mother, social class VII, father social class VI, Acre Lane), when asked about parents' evening and the kind of information she received there, replied:

> Some obviously could do a lot more because in a sense, I mean you can't sort of say very much to the teachers because they're tied for time be-

cause they've got so many parents to see...But I think they could do with a lot more you know and sort of give you an hour or something. I know it sounds a lot but to really get down and ask all the questions you want to ask because you don't get all the questions in that you want to ask...

Crozier (1999a) argues that teachers distance themselves from parents in order to protect their professional domain and thus their position of power, and Connell *et al.* (1982) suggest that the 'professional ideology' of teachers ' draws a boundary around what they are experts on' (p.130). Part of this process may be the failure by teachers to inform parents specifically about their children's academic progress and to provide details of the work that they cover – this would enable parents to help their children more, which they said they would welcome (Crozier, 1999a).

There are, however, as Wallman (1978, cited in David *et al.*, 1993) points out, two sides to the boundary; and the people on the different sides of it may interpret the boundary differently and for their own purposes. Drawing on Aldous (1978) and Ribbens (1990) David *et al.* indicate that maternal discourses, for example, demonstrate an interest in boundary creation and maintenance of the family unit. Evidence of this was apparent in this study as illustrated by parents' comments on their own and the teachers' different roles:

They've [the teachers] got their job to do, a parent has their job to do...We've both got our place...This is my area; this is my space. So you know it's my set of standards or our set of standards and that's how we do it here. I don't know that working with the school in any close way would make any difference in that... (Mrs Horn, year 7 mother, social class III, father social class IV, Acre Lane; quoted in Crozier, 1999a)

Just as Bourdieu *et al*'s (1994) university students hid behind the boundary of the formal lecture because it was safe and it enabled them to avoid undesirable threatening involvement, so too the working class parents could be said to take the same stance here.

Most parents, as others have also found (McClelland *et al.*, 1995), said that they did not want to be involved in the decision-making aspects of the school. However, those parents who were involved in the PTA, curriculum evenings, the parents' forum at Acre Lane or the school governing body, were with one or two exceptions middle-class. All parents irrespective of class gave a variety of reasons why they did not want to participate on committees or in the PTA. Many of these reasons included the demands of other commitments which will be discussed below. However, working-class parents explained that by and large they felt that these types of meetings were not for them. For example Mr Moss (year 9 father, social class IV, mother, social class unwaged homeworker, Acre Lane) explained: 'I'm not involved at all...with governors or nothing like that. I never have really bothered about that because I suppose it's just not in us' (quoted in Crozier, 1999a).

And Ms Reading (year 9 mother, social class III, lone parent, Acre Lane) explained:

> ...if they have a fete on or anything else like that, I will go along and help. I don't like getting involved with those committees because I don't enjoy them. I feel...there's too much resistance [conflict] on them...it's not my cup of tea. (Quoted in Crozier, 1999a)

The working-class parents at Brightside said similar things. Talking about whether she attended the Parent Teacher Association meetings, one mother said: 'No. I find those sort of meetings very cliquey. You're either in or you're way on the outside and I always felt myself on the outside, so I thought stuff it' (Mrs Foster, year 11 mother unwaged homeworker, father social class VI Brightside; quoted in Crozier, 1997) Another mother (Mrs Dyer, Year 7 mother, social class VII, father social class VI, Brightside) said: 'I'm not the sort of person, you can tell by looking at me, I think, that I wouldn't be involved in, with the PTA ... I mean I do help occasionally at the school fete and that but I mean...' Marginalisation leads to a sense of hopelessness with respect to having a voice but also a sense of not wanting to have anything to do with those sorts of events or activities anyway, as expressed by parents when they said, 'It's not in us', 'It's not my cup of tea'; 'I'm not the sort of person to be involved'; 'I always felt myself on the outside, so I thought stuff it.'

Working-class mothers also frequently talked about 'pushy' parents who endlessly got involved in the school or were always going up to the school (see also Reay, 1998). Their stance of non-involvement could be said to be a refusal to being sucked in to this kind of behaviour and into the 'cliquey' meetings which they deplored. Moreover, David *et al.*

(1993) suggest that schools not only seek to control the nature of the relationship between parent and school but 'they may also seek to shape parents' own view of themselves in terms of how they should define themselves as parent-educators, and how they should fulfil such a role' (pp14-15). As Mrs Foster (year 11 mother, social class unwaged home-worker, father social class VI, Brightside) put it when she was asked what she thought the school expected of her: 'To be a 'yes' man.' And she added, 'And I'm not.'

Rather than 'resigned submission', which suggests a passive indifferent stance, these working-class parents could thus be said to be taking a resistant position: in effect working-class parents could be said to be 'penetrating'[1] (Willis, 1977) the competitiveness amongst parents resulting from the market imperatives that the school has been forced into operationalising. The parents have not rejected the education on offer for their children, but they refuse to participate in the role of 'pushy parent', because they know it doesn't work for them anyway. On the occasions when they did intervene they often found that it was not worthwhile; they were not listened to (see also Vincent *et al.*, 2000). Mrs Foster for example had tried to get Brightside to take a more lenient attitude towards her son's black trainers which she had just bought for him instead of leather shoes. She replied in answer to what the school's response was: 'School rules, rules are rules' 'Rules are there to be obeyed' – talk to yourself time...waste of time, waste of breath.' And Mrs McClelland (year 9 mother, social class IV, father social class IV, Acre Lane) explained her experience of trying to get the teachers to change their views: 'They always seem to go back the way they want to do it anyway...you could shout and scream till the cows come home: if they weren't interested they weren't interested' (quoted in Crozier, 1999a).

Networking – social capital accumulation

Currently there are at least three discipline related explanations for social capital: those of sociology, political science and economics (Gamarnikow and Green, 1999). It is the sociological explanation that I am concerned with here. According to Coleman (1998) social capital can be defined in terms of its function:

> It is not a single entity but a variety of different entities with two elements in common: they all consist of some aspect of social structures, and they facilitate certain actions of actors... within the structure. Like other forms of capital, social capital is productive, making possible the achievement of certain ends that in its absence would not be possible...social capital may be specific to certain activities (p.82).

With respect to this last point, social capital may be valuable in one set of circumstances but harmful in another (*ibid.*). Coleman goes on to say that social structures and social relations facilitate the acquisition of social capital, and one explanation of the development of social capital is through the family and through a variety of community networks which also include the school. In Coleman's terms, and also according to Bourdieu and Passeron (1977), social capital contributes to a student's educational achievement. Likewise Lareau (1997) has argued that parents hold different sets of social resources and social relationships and this makes a difference to home-school relationships. Through social networks, middle-class parents are able to build up appropriate knowledge to facilitate the formation of a home-school relationship congruent with the schools' definition of it (p.713).

The middle-class parents in this study demonstrated their ability to acquire social capital in relation to school through their various networks, contacts and activities. Parents explained how their involvement in the Parent Teachers Association or other activities increased their understanding of the way the school works, and how their contact with other parents could lead to 'intelligence' gathering.

> I've been involved in the PTA which actually makes more decisions than I thought they did... People think all it does is raise money but I've actually learnt a lot about the way the school works...I've learnt more about the way the school works and just little things through staff, just sitting in the room where they have the meetings and reading things written on the board, that's quite illuminating (laughs) ...You do hear about things...and you meet other parents and then they feed in what they hear from their children. (Mrs Henderson, year 9 mother, social class II, father social class I, Brightside)

Also the more contact there is the more positive the relationship and implicitly the easier it is to hold a dialogue with teachers:

> The actual relationship at parents' evening works well because many of the teachers have taught one or more of our children so they know us. So there is no need to establish any particular rapport to start with....I know quite a lot of the members of staff; I'm involved in the Brightside School Trust. I meet one or two outside socially so they know me personally. So that obviously helps break down any barriers there might be. (Mr Darby, year 11 father; social class II, mother social class II, Brightside)

Whilst most working-class parents, had no knowledge of the school governors, middle-class parents spoke of the ways you could meet members of the governing body: for example, Mrs Higgins (year 11 mother, social class II, father social class I, Brightside) explained that she met them on the various committees she had served on. The significance of this contact can be demonstrated by the fact that governors canvassed parental opinion over the telephone, but tended to ring up only parents they knew. Moreover, once you are known you continue to get asked to be involved in school activities:

> I was on the Parent Teacher Association as a committee member. I was involved in helping with the Autumn fair; once your name is known you get called in. I've been on a couple of sub-committees. I was on one on special educational needs. (Mrs Higgins, year 11 mother, social class II, father social class I, Brightside)

This also links in with teachers at Brightside inviting in parents they knew, to speak on topics about which they had expertise.

Not only does this contact, albeit unwittingly, raise the profile of these parents and create the impression that they are interested, committed, 'motivated' and involved, but it provides further opportunities for them to develop networks, and this allows them to gain greater educational knowledge and understanding. Some parents deliberately endeavour to gain 'insider knowledge, as one parent explained:

> I get a lot of inside information from the librarian. Not intentionally, not at all, but we chat. That's usually why I help in school because I just like to hear what's going on and what they say about members of staff. It gives you a general picture of the school. (Mrs Shearer, year 9 mother, social class III, father social class I, Brightside; quoted in Crozier, 1997)

The more information the parents had the better placed they were to serve the needs and interests of their children. Sometimes they gained this information from their contacts or networks, or else they were on the 'inside' themselves. Mrs Money (year 7 mother, social class II, father social class II, Brightside) explained how this helped them choose their son's school: 'The most predominant reasons are the fact that we had the inside information with my husband working there – he's a teacher and also a governor as well.' She went on to say that she had been a parent governor at the infants' school and that her motivation for doing so was to gain 'insider information'. 'The best way to get involved is to find out what is really going on...You see the issues a bit more widely as to what the school is trying to do rather than just, you know, 'is the school meeting my needs?''

Working-class parents by contrast did not know the teachers socially nor did they tend to have access to others with educational knowledge, or at least not the same level of educational knowledge. Ms Reading (year 9 mother, social class III, lone parent, Acre Lane), when asked if she had voted in the election of the parent governors, explained: ' I don't know the people anyway. I mean I wouldn't know which one to pick ...'

Working-class parents did seek intelligence about their children's education and the schools they attended. However, they tended to do this through 'grapevine knowledge' (Ball and Vincent, 1998). As Mrs Robson (year 9 mother, social class III, father social class VI, Brightside), explained:

> I think we are the kind of family who are just interested in the overall effect of Brightside and what we've heard word of mouth from other parents whose children have gone there because my sister's daughter went there, so we knew how she [the sister's daughter] was getting on but without getting too involved in what's going on.

Social capital generates more social capital. Without the networks it would be difficult to access the requisite information. The very nature of networks leads to spiralling: one piece of information, or one contact, leads to another. That is not to say that social capital is self-renewing; access to social capital through networks and regular contact with the teachers was available to some extent for working-class parents while their children were at primary school; but once they had moved to secondary school this contact was undermined (see also Connell *et al.*, 1982).

Time factors and other commitments and concerns

Whilst primary schools have been reported as erecting their own barriers to parental involvement (see Reay, 1998, and Vincent, 1996 for example) parents in this study frequently commented on how much more involved they had been with their children's primary school than they were with the secondary school, at Acre Lane in particular, and how much easier it had been:

> I don't have a lot to do with the school as such...it's not like the junior school. You sort of lose contact because the children travel there backwards and forwards [on their own] whereas you'd go up there [to the juniors] and you'd know teachers, whereas there [Acre Lane] they're just names. (Mrs Stanley, year 11 mother, social class III, father social class VII, Acre Lane)

> My involvement with the school has been minimal and I feel very guilty about that. I've noticed that when both my children were in infant school you have a lot of involvement...I work part-time so I haven't been able to go in and you know help in school. [I] did [in the past] all sorts of things with, um, fund raising activities and things like that...I did some classroom work with some teachers. Since she's been [at Brightside] I drop her at the bus stop in the morning and she comes home at night. (Mrs Hill, year 7 mother, social class II, father social class II, Brightside)

McKibbin *et al.* (1998) also found in their research in Australia that key features of this distancing were echoed by their respondents. These included 'the school wasn't just up the road', 'parents don't drop off or pick up children', and that there were no or fewer activities such as the school fete where they could 'all pull together' (p.92). What seems to be expressed here is an absence of community as well as the opportunity to become known to and familiar with key actors.

Parents talked about the size of the secondary school especially in comparison with the primary school, both in terms of geographical space and in terms of the impersonality of the institution. Mrs Black (year 11 mother, social class VI, widow, Acre Lane) said that she didn't have much contact with Acre Lane which was very different from the infant and junior schools her children went to. She went on to say:

> You don't expect the same contact apart from parents' evening or other special meetings that are called from time to time...I don't see how you could have [more contact] in such a big school as that...I think it would be difficult for the staff.

And Mrs Stores (year 7 mother, social class II, father social class III, Acre Lane) explained, 'I don't think the communication's as good as it is in primary school, you don't get the contact with the staff that you ... it's just not possible to have that sort of contact.'

Some middle-class parents who had attended the school governors' AGM or other meetings at the junior school had ceased to be involved once their children went to the secondary school. Mrs Marchant (year 7 mother, social class II, father social class I, Brightside), for example, thought it might be to do with the size of the school.

There were other factors too of a practical nature which involved the changing nature of women's employment once their child had reached secondary school and the contemporaneous rise in employment of women with children (Brannen and Moss, 1998), not least in response to changing governmental expectations (see David, 1993a). There are other gender-related factors too which again are frequently intersected by social class and economic issues, for example the apprehension some women have about walking out alone at night, or not having access to transport. For this, some women were reliant on their partners; but they could not always accommodate this need because of their in-flexible work patterns. Other women just did not have transport.

> I don't go up [to the school] and they don't contact me...I would like to participate more with you know the different things that they do at school. But [Bob's] on shift work, so it always works, now like next Wednesday they've got a thing in school and it always works out that he's not around and if he's not around, I haven't got a car. (Mrs Sweep, year 9 mother, social class III, father social class VI, Acre Lane)

> It's a bit difficult to get down there. I do when it's time to see the teachers, make a special effort but there are no buses in the evening that go anywhere near the school... so it means either walking, it would be

about a three quarters of an hours walk... (Mrs Black, year 11 mother, social class VI, widow, Acre Lane)

Mrs Black also said that she didn't go to social events: 'The fact that I'm a widow makes it more difficult; when you go out socially you need someone to go with.'

As David (1993a) and Reay (1998), for example, have argued, parent-school involvement is predominantly 'women's work'. Women also continue to be mainly responsible for childcare generally. For many women who had children in different schools, supporting them with their various school tasks and keeping in contact with the schools, especially where resources were scarce, proved to be difficult. Although Ms Tasker may be exceptional, her situation is illustrative of this:

I've got six children. I can't be here, there and everywhere. I mean it's hard for me to spend like fifteen minutes a day on each child and concentrate on each child ...and when they come home from school and you say, 'What school work have you done, what have you done at school today?' And by that time its teatime and then it's like bedtime. (Ms Tasker year 9 mother, social class III, lone parent, Acre Lane)

As Phillips (1991) points out, there are two key problems with participatory democracy (read here parental involvement); one of these is 'its failure to recognise the additional burden on women's time' (p.44).

Conclusion

Parent-school relationships were therefore influenced by a combination of factors, experiences and perceptions which serve to encourage or deter involvement. In some cases the conditions were particularly conducive to involvement, whilst in other cases parents preferred relative independence from the school, perceiving the strategies by the school as implicating them in something not quite acceptable to them or else as placing them in a position which they found uncomfortable. Where people do not have access to making their 'voice heard' then they will take action into their own hands. These layers of influence are not therefore deterministic. The working-class parents here do have a sense of agency and as has been seen, they employ strategies themselves to wrest some control from the school, even though their 'actions' are considered by teachers as inaction and indifference.

The teachers are obviously key players in the parent-school relationship. In the following chapter their views on the parents' involvement, and the impact they feel it has on them, will be presented.

Notes

1   'Tiering' at GCSE level is a form of differentiation through group setting. At the time of the research (this has now changed) there were three tiers for mathematics: foundation, intermediate, and higher. Each tier only permitted a student to gain a certain grade so that in foundation level for mathematics it was only possible to gain a maximum D grade; at intermediate level it was only possible to gain a maximum C grade and at higher it was only possible to gain an A-C. If a student started off in a foundation group it was unlikely that s/he would be able change groups subsequently, as s/he would not have covered the necessary work appropriate for the other levels.

2   Like Apple (1995) I am wary of employing this term 'penetration', with its sexual and masculinist connotations implying, for example, male domination.

Chapter 5

Managing the parents:
the teachers' perspective

Introduction

Following the Plowden Report of 1967 parental involvement, whilst recommended as something which should be developed, was optional both for schools and for parents. At the start of the twenty-first century this is clearly no longer the case. The imperatives of the market, and also the drive to improve standards and meet targets, requires schools to draw in parents to support them in these endeavours. Through the pressures brought to bear by schools, parents, whether they want to or not, are expected to comply with the monitoring and support of their children. Some parents, as indicated in the account here, welcome this increased opportunity, although it is likely that such parents always wielded their power if they felt the need to do so (see for example Hatton, 1985; Birenbaum-Carmeli, 1999). But if other parents, as discussed in previous chapters, have attempted to respond to the expectation of parental involvement they have been obstructed; or else they have, in any case been intent upon resisting it, at least in the terms prescribed. It is likely though that pressure on these parents will increase as schools need to ensure the successful implementation of their home-school agreements.

In any event parents have become a central concern for schools and as such need to be managed. A central feature of schools is the maintenance of harmonious relations: amongst the students, between students and staff and now between parents and teachers (Everard and Morris, 1996). The different orientations of parents, as already recounted, pose particularly challenging demands on the teachers. To take this further, Gutmann (1999) says that the professionalism of teachers 'serves as a safeguard against repression and discrimination' (p.88) or at least it should, in the sense that teachers, as professionals, have a responsibility to safeguard the academic needs and general welfare of the young people in their charge and are accountable to others for executing this duty.

However, Lawn and Ozga (1988) have argued that professionalism is a complex concept and is one that changes according to the locations of teachers, the contradictions they embody, the different conditions in which they work and 'the social movements in which they are involved' (p.82). In other work I also have shown that teachers occupy different professional discourses which are at times contradictory (Crozier, 1996). Contradictory discourses of professionalism are present in this study too. These can be identified[1] as: 'professionalism as protectionism', in which teachers seek to defend their position, close ranks and maintain or reinforce the boundary between themselves and the external world; 'professionalism as critical response', to the market imperatives impinging on them; and 'professionalism as ethical response', where teachers' sense of fairness (in the face for example of more powerful parents) and professional integrity come into play. This chapter presents the teachers' views of the parents and their involvement, together with the implications of parental involvement for their professionalism. These different discourses are implicit or explicit in these views.

How is it for you? The teachers' views on parental involvement

To some extent the teachers' views on parental involvement have permeated the book so far. However, these have been expressed in response to the issues I have foregrounded. In this section I want to look at the teachers' views in their own right.

As already indicated, both parents and teachers described the parent-school relationship as 'very good' at Brightside and 'good' to 'fairly good' at Acre Lane. However, these platitudes rather mask the frustrations, tensions and even anxieties that teachers felt about the relationship.

These problems stemmed from different factors at the two schools. At Brightside, as has been seen, teachers were challenged by the demands of powerful parents, although there was a degree of harmony which stemmed from the 'match' or interconnectedness between parent and school/teacher; at Acre Lane teachers often felt frustrated by what some described as parental 'apathy' or inertia. In the following sections, therefore, I outline separately the views of the teachers from the two schools.

Brightside

> The PTA is very strong and they do a lot of fund-raising activities to sort of provide extra equipment, things that we wouldn't be able to afford otherwise. I think if parents came along on school visits that sort of thing, sort of helping in that way, would be good to see. I mean there are parents on the Curriculum Board and so when decisions are made about the curriculum parents are invited; parents are always invited if there are to be changes in the curriculum. Parents are invited in to find out exactly what the options are, what the possibilities are with each option, how to guide their children and I think that's important, so they can support their kids to make the right decision for them...(Head of year key stage 3)

The impression of involved, and in particular visible, parents is pervasive at Brightside. Moreover, teachers frequently spoke not only about the involvement of parents and the support they received, but also about the close relationship they had with many of the parents. These views bear out those of the parents recounted earlier, in particular about the sharing of perspectives on the educational endeavour and how to achieve the best for their children.

> I know a lot of parents quite well and that sort of relationship you build up also builds up quite a lot of trust and they do feel that they can phone up and they can ask anything you know...but it would probably come from a small number of very articulate, very aware parents who are probably in the education world themselves who have something specific to say and they really do know what they're talking about...they've got access to all the educational information and all the SATs material and all that sort of thing. (Subject head)

The teachers talked about the trust that many parents had in them and how important this was. It was important because it demonstrated agreement about, or at least acceptance of, what they did and in effect amounted to a vote of confidence, as well as an endorsement of their professional authority. They also described how they built up trust by providing information about the courses their children were doing. In the contemporary climate trust in professionals and those in authority is significantly diminishing. The development of self-helpism and the availability of information through publications, helplines and the Internet is one source of this but also the emphasis on surveillance and 'whistle blowing' is another. To build up trust amongst parents, as these teachers were endeavouring to do, could be seen as another device for binding them in. To trust is to rely on the judgement of another. Angela McRobbie[2] in a recent television discussion, argued that to refute trust can be politically empowering in that it can lead to the creation of alternative systems, behaviours, and solutions, just as the questioning by feminists of doctors led to the creation of the Our Bodies as Ourselves movement and well-woman clinics in the 1970s and 1980s.

The 'very articulate parents' who 'have something specific to say' can be engaged with. There can be some interaction. Communication with those who are not 'articulate' is, from the teachers' perspective, more problematic and may imply a lack of trust: 'With the less aware parents, the communication is very much one way from the school' (the same subject head quoted above).

Working-class parents here were considered frustrating. They did not fulfil the expectations; they did not seem to be meeting their part of the 'bargain'. There was some attempt by teachers to try to understand from the parents' perspective the constraints they might be under, but as in the example below, the teachers' sentiments were frequently tinged with a derogatory perception.

> I think a lot of them have just got the idea that they send their kids to school and we should sort out the school stuff and that's our job. Sometimes I think it's economics, you know they work, and it's too difficult to get an evening off. Some of them I think it's complete disorganization and no real communication between parent and child. (Head of year key stage 4)

Although there was a strong sense of understanding between the majority of the middle-class parents and the teachers, there were still disagreements and disjunction. According to some of the teachers there was a sizeable liberal element amongst the parents which did not wholly espouse the values of the school with respect for example to school rules. There were various disagreements over school uniform and whilst this was an issue for the working-class parents, too, the root cause was significantly different. For the working-class parents the disagreement lay in the fact that they had only limited resources; for example, they could only afford one pair of shoes and so bought something which they hoped their child could wear both in and out of school, such as black trainers – but then found this was not permissible. The middle-class parents, were either uninterested in school uniform and did not particularly encourage the wearing of it or they would support their child's expression of her/his individuality, for example in the wearing of a nose stud. This was a source of annoyance for teachers:

> I mean school dress is one example that's a bugbear here. It's immensely helpful if parents say, 'Yes, I'll put up with the concept of having some functional school dress and I'll ensure that my child wears it.' Whereas if a parent says, 'I disapprove. I think it's quite acceptable my child comes to school with a nose stud and green training shoes', then that becomes an issue; it's difficult for everybody you know, it's energy-sapping, time-wasting stuff, fighting over who gets to have their way about it and whether that child's made an exception of or not. (Head of year key stage 3)

There was a similar issue around a local pop festival for which these liberal parents allowed their children to take time off school. So whilst there was substantial sharing of educational values, there was a mismatch in a number of respects which created some dissonance.

The role of 'policing' is very time-consuming for teachers and detracts from what they feel they can do best and want to do most. Their expectations of parents includes wanting their help in ensuring that the right conditions for teaching and learning are created. School-uniform adherence, accepting school rules generally and behaviour are all aspects of these 'right' conditions. Given that middle-class parents seemed to share similar understandings on education and pedagogy with the teachers, this rift seemed all the more perverse.

However, middle-class parents had three advantages to compensate for this situation. Two are related to their relative power position: one is their articulacy (their voice – Hirschman, 1970) in that they can effectively defend their stance and their child's behaviour, and the second is that they also have the power of exit (ibid.). Of course all parents in theory have this power but as research has shown with respect to choosing schools, middle-class parents are much more likely to exert it (Gewirtz *et al.*, 1995). The third advantage relates to the credibility they gain from their high visibility as 'involved' parents. This compares with working-class parents, who tend not to be visible except when there is a difficulty to sort out and who are thus generally regarded less favourably. If they send their children to school in the 'wrong' shoes then this just reinforces the negative view of them as uncooperative parents.

Acre Lane

The kinds of expectation teachers have of the parents have already been described in chapter 3. In many respects the teachers at Acre Lane, felt that the vast majority of parents were not giving them the kind of support they wanted. Below are indicative comments from teachers on this issue.

> ...with those parents who are involved – very good, excellent...There's very few parents who will actually come up and get involved, I've got to say that... the biggest problem is that the number of parents who do actively involve themselves is very small... there is a great inertia out there from the parents I come into contact with...(Head of year 3)

> There's a hard core of parents who are supportive to the school, interested in education, critical as well. Then there's the middle group who don't want to know, probably comprises 60 per cent of the school's population. The ones who are very supportive probably comprise 10 per cent of the school's population. So there's about 30 per cent who will attend all parents' evenings, will only go and see English and Mathematics teachers and will support the school where they feel its in their child's interests. (Subject head).

There was also a strongly held view that the majority of these 'unsupportive' and 'uninvolved' parents were indifferent, and unmotivated. Some teachers thought that it was a problem endemic to that part of the city, a predominantly working-class area which had lost its main source of employment and was now, experiencing pockets of financial hardship.

> A lot of parents just don't want to be involved. A lot of the parents did not have a good experience of education themselves, perhaps at the same school. They believe that education did not do them any good. That it was irrelevant to their needs and they share the same view about education for their children as well; that it's something to be endured and therefore they will keep away as much as possible. Now that's one group and I think that's the majority group. (Subject head)

Whilst the teachers' analysis of the working-class parents' own educational experience did in some respects resonate with what the parents also said, their view of these parents as seeing education as irrelevant was not manifested at all in the views the parents expressed to us. By contrast, as already indicated, the working-class parents valued their children's education highly, seeing it as an opportunity, and a necessity for improving their life chances.

Connell *et al.*'s (1982) study in Australia of the impact of class on children's education, also recounted the misperceptions between teachers and working-class parents. Connell *et al.* argued that teachers' criticisms of working-class parents and their perception of them as for example 'incompetent' did not stem from an anti-parent attitude, but illustrates the class-based nature of the parent-teacher relationship. They go on to say that in a school where most of the parents have less education than the teachers and lack 'educational knowledge', as well as being on lower incomes, the teachers are more able to assert their professional ideology (p.130). As this subject head indicates, 'Here at [Acre Lane] to a certain extent you can do what you like and only a few parents would complain if there was any come-back...'

Hoy and Miskel (1989) argue that school managers employ 'inter-organisation coping strategies', for example by establishing 'favourable linkages with important external constituencies and shaping environmental elements...' By doing this, school managers can, they say, reduce 'the environmental uncertainty' (p.44). The management of Acre Lane can be seen to operate in this way: driven on by pressures to raise the profile and performance of the school and to demonstrate to Ofsted, for example, that they are making efforts, at least, to develop good home-school relations, the senior management of the school tended to be up-beat about parental involvement. An example of this was their continuing efforts to draw parents into the school through different strategies such as the Parents' Forum (even though this was mainly aimed at the middle-class parents). The class teachers and middle managers, however, expressed a sense of resignation or even despair about ever involving the majority of parents.

> In one sense as a school our expectations of parents probably could be described as being realistic or perhaps even cynical...if you realise the amount of effort put in for disproportionately low results then the effort tends to go elsewhere. (Subject teacher Acre Lane)

Their analysis of the working-class parents covered not only their poor educational background and economic circumstances but also suggested that some parents were negative, uncooperative and at times difficult in their relations with the school.

> I have a feeling that quite a lot of parents if they see a letter from the school they won't open it or [they] throw it in the bin or file it but they won't act on it. I also think that the reading skills on that letter are quite high and that the parents find it quite difficult to access the information from that letter and that it will be shelved for that reason. (Subject head.)

> There are some parents you'd definitely want to have on your side. Parents described as 'tricky customers', if not on your side you'd get a sore ear. (Subject teacher)

> Some parents are known on the teacher grapevine that you can't count on their support...so I wouldn't ask for it. (Subject teacher)

> Some, a minority, downright refuse to allow their children [to have a detention], others don't cooperate, others appear to be inaccessible. Often there's parental backing but I understand that often the parents are quite powerless as well. (Same subject teacher as above)

Just as the parents said, the teachers at Acre Lane had limited relations with them. Unlike the teachers at Brightside, these teachers did not on the whole know the parents socially.

> ...with most of the parents of the children I teach my relationship is tenuous, almost non-existent. But when there is a relationship it's polite and short, in some cases it's cordial, fruitfully in one sense it's affirming, to each other, that we are interested in the child. (Subject teacher)

As the parents said, they felt less inclined to come into the school and talk to the teachers, partly because they did not know them. Likewise the teachers not knowing most of the parents who also seemed to them to have a different way of behaving, failed to understand them and consequently mistrusted them (see also Connell *et al.*, 1982)

Teachers at Acre Lane had a clearly demarcated class analysis of the different parent groups in their school, although they did not always express it in class terms. And once again, just as it has been seen with the Brightside teachers, it is in relation to those parents with whom they can identify or who identify, with them, that there is a responsiveness:

Parents who are involved in their children's education in an active way who are usually more highly educated, um – more middle-class – are aware of the concept of things like target setting, will go into detail and think about it and take notice and all the rest of it and are capable of reflection and evaluation...And there are parents whose experience of school was really negative who do not feel that school is a positive thing and they're sort of at the other end of the spectrum...I don't think they generally don't cooperate because they don't really see any point, they don't see the need. They don't really – um – they're not active reflecting people – um- [they're] generally less educated and less cooperative and don't have any real interaction with the school. (Subject teacher) (Quoted in Crozier, 1998)

The parents that come [to parents' evening] tend to be the parents of children who are succeeding anyway...the one's that do care get more involved as they [the students] progress because of the looming exam situation. (Subject teacher)

A motivated parent is a parent that is interested in their child, talks to them, that knows where they are in the evening that helps the children be equipped for lessons, that shows some interest in what the pupils are learning, that would take them to the library and provide them with the bus fare; would look at their homework; would just be interested in them. (Subject teacher) (Quoted in Crozier, 1998)

There have been parents who have been fantastic, who have backed me up all the way down the line... and even advising me as to the best way to approach their child, but they have to be articulate in order to do that, they have to be of a relatively sort of ...understanding, I suppose, and of a certain sort of intelligence... Some parents... have very poor parenting skills... (Subject teacher)

It is very clear from this what sort of parent these teachers value. There is also concerningly a negative stereotyping and prejudicial view of working-class parents. Implicit in the views expressed here is a sense of superiority on the part of the teachers. As indicated in chapter 1, there is also the notion of the 'good' parent, and the 'bad' parent, which has been well documented (see for example Vincent, 1996). The 'good' parent *inter alia*, as Vincent (1996) points out, 'has an overtly positive attitude towards the school and encourages the same in the child' (p.92); 'the good parent also behaves in a particular way in the school' – displaying appropriate behaviour, that is according to the teacher's definition (pp.93-4). Vincent also points out that the concept is highly gendered, given that the majority of active parents are mothers. Hence the incompetent parent with poor parenting skills in effect means mothers.

As seen in Chapter 3, where parents and teachers meet socially, or parents' views on their child, or on educational practice match those of the teacher, then there ensues a profitable relationship for the child. This seems to be confirmed from the teachers' perspective too. Teachers said that they related differently to parents who they felt were on 'their side':

> There are other parents whose children I am interested in and I tend to be interested in their parents and as a result because I'm motivated if you see a parent who is clearly anxious or concerned or supportive, then even after all these years there is a glow, a feeling that they are worthy, decent people and they value education and it's right and proper that you make an effort for them and their children. (Subject teacher)

These negative views of the parents espoused by the majority of the teachers (senior managers were more understanding of their parent body and less dismissive) did not match the attitudes from the Acre Lane working-class parents we interviewed, as outlined already. Teachers' perceptions of parents' apparent absence or invisibility leads to this negative view of them. Parents' absence was, as has been seen, caused by a variety of factors including a resistance to being drawn into a role which is defined, as argued above, solely on the teachers' terms, also a refusal to be placed in a position where they are made to feel uncomfortable and inadequate. If teachers hold these views of the parents it is little wonder that the parents feel reluctant to go into the school.

Teachers' professionalism

According to Gutmann (1999), notwithstanding the reference to teachers' 'safeguarding' role referred to earlier, the professional autonomy of teachers is often invoked to curb the influence of school students on their own education. This could also be said to happen with parents. The professionalism of teachers can serve to set them apart, and can act as a defence or buffer against the interference or disparagement of parents. On another level, it is the professionals who have to take ultimate responsibility for it is they who are accountable and as Hoyle and John (1995) assert 'being accountable, entails being responsible' (p.110). It is, therefore, they who are or should be concerned about the interests of the whole of the school community, unlike parents who are self-interested in terms of their own child.

As Le Grand (1996) (cited in Whitty, 1997b) has observed, during the 'golden age of teacher control from 1944 to the mid 1970s (Lowe, 1993) parents and children were expected to trust the professionals and accept that teachers knew what was best for [the] children' (Whitty, 1997b, p303). This position has now been radically challenged and teachers not only find their authority questioned but also they are frequently criticised. It is thus likely that teachers would invoke their professionalism to defend themselves against the sustained criticisms that were levelled against them throughout the Conservative administration and subsequently under New Labour as well. They also have to shield themselves from ongoing criticisms in the media (Ozga, 2000) which have a wider affect than government criticisms –though these too are fuelled by government ministers or the Chief Inspector for Schools. Accountability has taken on a potentially more sinister stance than hitherto especially as it is going to be linked to pay and status increases; this together with OFSTED inspections leads teachers to 'play the game' and comply with the standard format of performance indicators and competencies. Indeed, as Woods and Jeffrey (1996) have argued, 'accountability is a principle feature of the new professional managerialism', which in turn is a device to help operationalise the education (quasi-) market and the competition between schools. Such requirements in themselves serve to undermine teachers' professionalism, as has the National Curriculum and other statutory prescriptions, which are dictating to teachers how they should to do their job (see for example Ball, 1993; Hughes, 1997). Parents telling them what to do could be seen as the last straw.

It is not surprising then if tension is created between teachers and parents as a result of the discourses of consumerism and accountability (see also Jonathan, 1990), and leads to the teacher asserting her/his 'authority' and the view that s/he is right.

> I think we bend over backwards to accommodate parents but if it is an enquiry about a member of staff, I try and put the point of view that the member of staff must be right really, but knowing full well that sometimes we're not angels and I try to sort it within the establishment ...[I] give them a rational explanation but not always the explanation which I know to be factually correct ... I mean that's pretty rare, maybe twice a year you might get something like that. They're always dealt with, if it's a complaint about a teacher it's dealt with but it's not necessarily dealt with openly with the parent... (Head of year key stage 4, Acre Lane)

> I've known situations where parents come in and expect you to drop everything to deal with them and I won't do that, I refuse as a matter of professional principle to do that because I say to the parent, 'You wouldn't expect to go along to the doctor's surgery and expect them to drop everything and come and see you. You wouldn't go along to a solicitor's office and expect them to drop everything and come and see you?' So I will not do that... (Another Head of year key stage 4, Acre Lane)

These teachers' comments indicate their desire to protect their professionalism by closing ranks and reinforcing the boundary on the one hand, and by asserting their authority in general on the other. Perhaps more poignantly, teachers were adamant about holding onto their pedagogic authority too.

> If there's a problem in the family, say a grandparent has died and they don't want the child to do a unit on bereavement in RE the next week or something, I think that's fair enough because they're self-selecting for their child. But I think I'd object if somebody came in and said that you're teaching this all wrong and you don't know what you're talking about, because I feel I do and I spent four years at University learning how to do it. (Head of year key stage 3, Brightside)

> I think it's interesting to hear their views, but I think everyone thinks they're experts on education just because they went to school. (Another Head of year key stage 3 Brightside)

Not all the teachers in the two study schools responded in a defensive way about their professionalism, but when they were asked if they would change what they were doing if a parent questioned their practice they then asserted their professionalism.

At both schools teachers said that they would rarely change their practice or curriculum content (where they still had any control left over this) or decisions about setting for example, in response to a parents' concerns. However, at Brightside this appears to have happened more often than at Acre Lane, at least according to the parents' responses. Again this is class- and power-related and connected to the greater likelihood of the teachers at Brightside and the middle-class parents at the school sharing a view about education and the needs of the child. Therefore it is unsurprising that such occasions were less frequent at Acre Lane. For example, in response to a question about whether he had changed any particular practices as a result of parents' interventions, this teacher from Acre Lane replied:

> Very rare, could be a matter of some shame. I suppose the most profound impact would be the parent who you see is likely to be pushy or to make further enquiries or to check work that I as an individual would make sure I'd mark scrupulously, step up my discourse with the child involved, so I could be seen to be responding. In one sense that satisfies the parent and I as a parent myself with kids at another comprehensive school, I've seen how that works because you pressurise the teacher and your child gets a relative advantage because the teacher is going to respond – not necessarily for disinterested or worthy reasons but as a matter of professional protection. (Subject teacher, Acre Lane)

Other teachers spoke about how they would eschew parents' demands – and not always through very professional means; for example this teacher explained in response to a question about changing practice:

> No I don't think I would... What I might do, I don't think I've ever done it, but probably what I would do if they were really bolshy is re-describe what I would do so that it sounded responsive... which is terrible really because its like I think I'm right but I probably would (laughing). I think that's probably what would happen, yeh lie to some extent... (subject teacher, Acre Lane)

'Professional protection' can be seen to be a significant feature in the parent-school relationship and part of the process of managing the parents which as I said earlier was central to teachers' professional practice and concerns. The examples presented above are of teachers who may have made concessions but only where extreme pressure was exerted and when they felt under particular threat. The implication is clearly that such pressure is exerted by middle-class parents.

Teachers did recount incidents where the child and the parent were consistently unhappy, for example about a set change, and then the teacher may have agreed to the parent's wishes, but this they said was exceptional. It was also clearly as a result of the interventions of a tenacious and insistent parent, and one with whom the teachers identified:

> Sometimes if it is a difficult judgement and they're a parent who's clearly thought about it, sometimes they're a parent who has insider knowledge anyway. Obviously you're going to be more affected by, let's say, a parent who is a governor, who has some knowledge of education, who is questioning your judgement on something. Obviously that makes a big impact upon you and you think hard about it because you realise they are in a position to question you ... (Subject head, Brightside)

Powerful parents who achieved changes as a result of their interventions posed ethical dilemmas for some teachers. They did after all employ criteria based on assessment in making these decisions, and being consistent was a matter of maintaining fairness and equal opportunities. There was, however, evidence in both schools that the more 'powerful' parents could gain advantage at the expense of the less 'powerful'.

> I'm very aware, that a very small number of parents get a huge amount of the 'discussion cake', if you like, they're the one's who are always there with you know their demands and you've got to think, 'Hang on to the comprehensive school', and who is supporting the majority of kids who just aren't going to go on to university to do those things? (Subject head, Brightside)

> I mean I do feel a certain concern that the vocal minority can affect an awful lot of change in a school like this because we are so concerned with listening to parents and all you need is three parents to make a note like 'We think SATs are wonderful and we want you to spend more time teaching to the tests rather than...' you only need a few people to make

a fuss and the whole school would be jumping backwards to try to deal with that, whereas I think, 'Hang on a minute, we are the professionals'... (Subject head, Brightside) (Quoted in Crozier, 1997)

The head of key stage 4 at Acre Lane was also very clear about this potential problem. In answer to a question about whether parents questioned what the school or the teachers were doing he replied:

Yes some do, most don't. I mean the majority of parents don't take the opportunity to do that...Those that do tend to be the, um, what shall I say, the more articulate parents who feel a certain ability to make those sort of comments and those sort of judgements. And we'll listen to them and act or react accordingly. The danger is, in something like that, is that almost inevitably it's a minority of parents. I mean it's dangerous to take action on the basis of a minority viewpoint, you know, just because somebody takes the time to comment adversely or positively about some aspects of the school's operation doesn't necessarily mean that's representative of all parents' views.

In her study of parents in Tel Aviv, Birenbaum-Carmeli (1999) demonstrated the oppressive impact of a group of powerful parents both on teachers and also on the less powerful working-class parents. As she says,

...the realisation of the democratic civil rights by privileged groups, may turn into a silencing of other voices. Thus weaker groups whose interests do not coincide with those of the powerful and who are economically, socially or culturally unable to exercise their civil rights, may find that their relative condition has deteriorated...(p.86)

As can be seen here, on occasions maintaining fairness got caught up with responding to the market and 'keeping parents happy'. Teachers were conscious of the competition between schools for students and some were quite angry at the pressures this imposed and its interference with their work.

I hate this marketing, market forces stuff which puts pressure on, 'we must have this number of children in and we must do this'. I really find that distracting. I think it puts more pressure on teachers; I think, you know, you don't need to oversell, overkill your school. I think you just need to, you can just continue to do the best you can do... (Subject teacher, Brightside)

This same teacher recounted an incident which had occurred that day while discussing the setting for the following year. One of her students had not done very well and she was going to be put into a lower set. This teacher made a plea for her on the grounds that it was only one test and that to put her down would undermine her confidence. The response she received was, 'How would we justify that [making an exception] to parents? Because if she stays up someone else will have to go down.' This teacher subsequently felt that her 'professional judgement is of no use'.

Ball (1990) has described the new managerialism in schools as being imported from industry. He outlines how, as in industrial management, school managers are set apart to take key decisions to the exclusion of the teachers, who in their turn are to be managed. He goes on, '...they [the teachers] are cast as lay persons with at best a residual right of consultation. In this assertive process influence over the definition of the school is removed to a great extent from the hands of teachers. [Moreover], within such a discourse the curriculum becomes a delivery system and teachers become its technicians or operatives.' (p.154)

Conclusion

Teachers, parents and students are all under some form of surveillance, frequently carried out by each other. As has become clear, this situation is hardly conducive to participatory, democratic partnership. Although on the surface the relationships between teachers and parents seem to be functional, there is an underlying unease, if not at times an antagonism. Teachers' professionalism seems to some extent to provide a safeguard for teachers under duress, but Giroux (1997) has argued that teachers' maintenance of this 'professionalism barrier' is both 'highly exclusionary and undemocratic' (p.111). It can also be seen here that there is a communications gap between the teachers and the working-class parents, in terms not simply of information-giving, but also of a lack of understanding on the part of the teachers of what the parents are about, what they want from education for their children, and what they do for their children away from the school. Underpinning this fissure are the negative views of this group of parents held by many of the teachers.

Of course there are two sides to the parent-teacher/school relationship, but in spite of the shifts in power relations that have been discussed, teachers are better placed than parents to take the initiative in addressing the constraints upon democratic, participatory partnership and weakening the boundaries. The discourses of 'professionalism as ethical response, fairness and integrity' together with 'professionalism as critical response', referred to in the introduction to this chapter and demonstrated subsequently, offer the potential for this change.

The other significant player in the parent-school relationship, the school student, has thus far had little mention. In the following chapter, the voices of students and their views on parental involvement in their education will be presented and discussed in order to display a more complete picture of the conditions necessary for building a democratic and participatory partnership.

1   I am grateful to Diane Reay for suggesting this typology of the different discursive levels of teacher professionalism and for making me aware of the need to foreground these professional discourses which are apparent in my analysis.

2   *Newsnight* BBC2 4 February 2000

Chapter 6

Whose life is it anyway? School students' views on parental involvement[1]

The policy emphasis in raising achievement and standards has been on school management and parental involvement; consequently, the voice of school students has been ignored. Whilst populist and educational discourses are concerned with individuality and rights, paradoxically educational policy seems to care little for the diverse needs of a heterogeneous student population (see also Jeffs, 1995). Failure to consider the student perspective seems to jar with the current interest in citizenship education. The Secretary of State for Education, David Blunkett, addressing the Citizenship Conference at the Institute of Education, (July 1999) about the proposals for citizenship education, indicated his view when he said:

> [pupils will] have the chance to exercise real responsibility and make an impact on the school and communities. We are seeking nothing less than the encouragement of active and responsible members of tomorrow's community. Offering time for voluntary activities and bringing alive democracy at a time when cynicism is rife, is a key objective. (DfEE, 1999)

This would seem to suggest that school students need to be involved and to participate fully in the life and functioning of their schools. At the present time, however, rather than setting in place the means by which young people can work towards becoming such responsible and 'active' citizens, there are, seemingly, excessive control measures placed upon them. The government's answer to those children and parents who apparently refuse to knuckle down and conform to prescribed requirements is a series of authoritarian measures: tagging of children from ten years upwards; curfews; for parents who can't 'control' their children, the possibility of having to attend parenting classes; if their child is a persistent truant, fines or courts orders to take the child to school each day. Little attention is being paid here to the different needs of the children or to the complexity of social interactions.

The successful achievement of the endless targets that central government has set for schools and LEAs alike, as well as for individual students is taking priority; and in order to achieve these targets, rather than freeing up the control structures, they are finding that they need to impose a tighter hold. Moreover, such control measures tend to demonise the children, which in turn infiltrates education policy. Speaking from a global perspective, Usher and Edwards (1994), suggest that developments in societies have resulted in the 'breakdown of established patterns of work and life', which can result in an increase of 'deviance, delinquency, and disorder' (p.203). Therefore they recognise the need for the management of these effects and the role of education in this management, with government intervention to ensure it:

> Governments' attitudes toward education are therefore governed by a desire to (re)establish (self-)discipline among learners, in order that they become and remain law-abiding citizens...this is dealt with by governments taking more control of what goes on in compulsory schooling... (p.204).

This echoes what I have said in previous chapters about the apparent need for different forms of control and strategies of surveillance, as a result of the deregulation of the education system. Parents are seen as central to fulfilling this role for example through parent contracts and the monitoring of homework, attendance and punctuality.

As Fine (1997) has argued parents are in this way being positioned 'as subjects but also as objects of a struggle to resuscitate the public sphere of public education' (p.460); they are expected to control and monitor the behaviour of their children, but scant regard is placed upon seeing them as equal partners with the school in their children's learning. In this way school students themselves are positioned as objects, perceived as the other and rendered silent with respect to their own educational experience.

In all the policy changes that have taken place in education over the past ten years, there has been little opportunity for the voice of the school student to be heard, and yet the policy changes impact most profoundly upon the students themselves. Moreover, with a few exceptions (such as Kinder *et al.*, 1996, Kinder *et al.*, 1997, the recent ESRC-funded research David *et al.*, 1998, and Flutter *et al.*, 1999) little research has been carried out into school students' views on their own educational experience and needs.

This chapter is an attempt to begin to give a voice to young people in relation to one aspect of policy: their views on the involvement of their parents in their schooling.

Talking Back[2]

The concern with school students' views on their parents' involvement arose from the three-year research project into parental involvement reported on in the previous chapters. As explained in the Introduction, there had not been an intention originally to look at students' views, but one of the key issues that emerged from the research into parent-school relationships was that parents said they would actively help their children more if they would let them, or if they expressed the desire for help more often. According to the parents, the older the child, the less they wanted their help. If these views were correct then, they could lead to a tension with the government policy of home-school agreements, the overseeing of homework, regular visits to schools and contact with teachers. Also, implicit in government policies on parental involvement is the view that parents are not sufficiently involved or don't want to be involved. The purpose of this strand of the research, therefore, was to ascertain students' views about their parents' involvement in their schooling. However, it was not possible to triangulate the responses from parents at Brightside and Acre Lane. A further school, Lowlands as already explained, was thus approached and a questionnaire was distributed at the end of the school year to 474 students from years 7, 8, 9 and 10. Year 11 students had left school by this time and a further 156 students were either on school visits or were absent on the day the questionnaire was distributed. The school had no sixth form. The questionnaire was distributed by the group tutor and completed in class time. The response rate is shown in Table 1.

Table I.

N=474	Percentage
Year 7	26% (124)
Year 8	27% (130)
Year 9	26% (122)
Year 10	21% (98)

Most of the questions were closed, although there was opportunity for the students to respond to some open questions in elaborating on their answers. Students were asked about parental support with homework, parents' attendance at parents' evenings and parental involvement in general terms. They were also asked some contextualising questions with regard to siblings, hobbies and interests, attitudes towards school, and their perceptions of their own academic progress and behaviour. Details of their parents' occupations were asked for in order to give some indication of their social-class locations.

In the following year, semi-structured interviews were carried out with 14 girls and 14 boys from year 7 and 20 boys and 20 girls from year 10: a total of 68 students. We interviewed them in single-sex and mixed-sex groups and on a one-to-one basis. We were unable to correlate their responses with those of the questionnaire, which had been completed anonymously, but most of the year 10 students would have completed it. Further details of the school are given in Appendix 1 and the research methods are discussed in Appendix 2.

This chapter presents a discussion of the key findings from the questionnaire responses and the interviews. The students' responses from Lowlands frequently mirrored the parents' responses from Acre Lane and Brightside, particularly those of the working-class parents, for example with respect to the nature of parental involvement, the level and type of communication from the school to the parent, their sense of trust that the school would identify any concerns about their progress, and their lack of intitiative in seeking information or in being proactive in their own learning.

Contextual Details

In the questionnaire the students were asked about their parents' occupation in order to shed some light on their social-class locations. 30 per cent did not reply regarding their mother's employment and 35 per cent did not reply regarding their father's employment. Tutors reported that in many cases students did not reply to this question, because they did not feel comfortable about doing so.

Using the Goldthorpe (1987) and Goldthorpe and Hope (1978) social-class categorisations, the parents' occupations were classified as outlined below:

Table 2

Mothers' Social-Class Categorisation	Percentage	N=474
I	0	
II	4	
III	22	
IV	0	
V	I	
VI	4	
VII	I6	
Unwaged homeworker	I8	
Unemployed	5	
Student	0	
Disabled from work	I	
Retired	I	

The majority of the students (94 per cent) said that they had or had had at least one brother or sister at the school.

Just under half of the students said that they liked school either *very much* or *quite a lot*; 35 per cent said they liked it *a little* while just under a quarter didn't like it at all. For almost 40 per cent their description of their behaviour ranged from *excellent* to *quite good* with only 4 per cent

Table 3

Fathers' Social-class categorisation	Percentage	N=474
I	0	
II	6	
III	4	
IV	12	
V	3	
VI	14	
VII	16	
Unwaged homeworker	1	
Unemployed	7	
Student	0	
Disabled from Work	1	
Retired	1	

saying that they *could do better*. The remainder did not reply. A similar response was received to the question concerning academic progress in all subjects. The majority did not respond, but those who did (40 per cent) were fairly positive.

Students were asked to write down three hobbies or interests. The majority (76 per cent) mentioned sport followed by roller-blading or bike riding (26 per cent). Socialising with friends (18 per cent) was also a popular pastime. Other hobbies or interests included the performing arts (14 per cent), watching television (12 per cent), computers (9 per cent), reading (7 per cent) and crafts (4 per cent). Fewer than 1 per cent mentioned holidays. Most of these activities were not surprisingly, done with friends (57 per cent) or alone (25 per cent), but 32 per cent said they did them with either friends or parents. Also 80 per cent referred to activities that they did with parents, with visiting relatives being the most predominant of these (35 per cent).

With regard to the more substantive issues, student responses appear to be influenced by a range of factors of which age, family circumstance, gender and school success or attitude to school seem to be of particular significance.

Whilst a common theme across all age groups was that students wanted parental support and approbation, year 10 students wanted it subject to certain conditions, one of which was having control, whilst year 7 students were more likely to seek it out, and accepted it in a much less conditional way. This came across very strongly in the interview responses. All the year 7 children, when interviewed on a one-to-one basis or in single-sex groups, said that they told their parents, but mainly their mothers, everything. This is borne out by other research which shows that most young people confide in and communicate with their mothers more than their fathers, where their father lives in the family home (see for example Anderson and Clarke, 1982; Buchanan *et al.*, 1991). The children spoke about telling their parents about when they had 'done something good' and wanting their parents to know about their school work. They were particularly keen to keep their parents informed, irrespective of whether their work was 'good' or 'bad'. The boys in mixed-sex interview groups were the exception to this since they said that they usually did not tell their parents if they were not doing well, or at least tried to keep it from them, although the girls in these groups tended to tell their parents.

> I do tell them because if you don't tell them they'll probably find out anyway. (Jeannette, year 7)

> I do tell them most of the time but it depends what mood my mum's in really. I try to make it that I tell her something bad and good at the same time. (Kelly, year 7)

> I'm quite lucky really because some people find it hard to tell their parents like bad things they have done and they find it difficult but I don't mind because me and my mum have got a really good relationship and we can talk to each other about anything. They won't have a go at me as long as I say that I've tried my hardest. (Sue, year 7)

Keith (year 7) said that he told his parents if he had done something 'good' at school and also if he had been in trouble because 'I always want to be honest with my parents.'

The gender differences in the students' responses (all year groups) to parental involvement in their schooling are difficult to separate out from their seemingly different relationships with their parents. These different relationships, it goes without saying, have a bearing upon the kind of support or involvement they want from their parents. Where there appears to be a more clearly indicated gender difference is in a tendency for girls to be more compliant and more accepting of the monitoring and control strategies. Indeed it could be said that girls have less to fear from being monitored, especially given that boys are four times as likely as girls to be excluded from school (Blyth and Milner, 1994). Boys are therefore more likely to be seen as troublesome and a threat and are consequently prime targets for surveillance.

As previously stated, the nature of the family structure influenced the home-school-student relationship. In keeping with social trends, our respondents' family structures were diverse, including lone parent mother; mother, step-father and siblings; father, step-mother and siblings; two older friends acting as guardians; foster parents; and the traditional two parents and siblings. Where the natural father did not live in the family home, then he was, whether intentionally or not, generally excluded from the school's day-to-day requirements of parents and from ongoing knowledge of how his daughter or son was progressing. As one girl, whose father and mother were divorced, said about a parents' evening attended by both natural parents, 'I think it's okay for my mum because my mum like knows how I'm getting on, but dad, he doesn't know really how much I get on with the school; so I think dad feels a bit uncomfortable.'

Although mothers were the most active parents with respect to school, this was not wholly the case. The mothers might be the main confidante, but seeking practical help with homework would depend on which parent, or other available adult or sibling, had the most knowledge or expertise. Where the child did not live with her/his natural father, the father might know less about the child's school work, but the child might take part in various social or leisure activities with the father, such as sport or going to the cinema. One boy explained that he made a point of finishing his homework before he went to stay with his father at the weekend because, he said, 'I don't usually take my bag and homework down my dad's' – in order to keep his time free to spend on other kinds of activity with his father.

The attitude of students to school was an important factor in deciding whether they wanted support from their parents or whether they wanted their parents to know about what they were actually doing or how they were getting on. According to their own responses, in both the questionnaire and the interviews, some students felt they were successful and were generally positive about school; others felt quite successful and were happy in school most of the time and others did not like school, and were discontented with most subjects. A small minority of students felt antagonistic towards school. I shall return to this issue below.

Parental Involvement

The parents, according to the students in the questionnaire sample, were barely involved in activities such as the PTA, fund-raising or helping in the school generally: a point which echoes my other findings, especially where the parents are working-class. However, in other respects they were involved in supporting their children in a variety of ways. Most of the students (92 per cent) felt happy with the amount of help they received. For example, 63 per cent said that their parents always or usually attended parents' evenings and only 11 per cent reported that their parents never did so. In the interviews, only one year 10 boy complained that his mother could have been more supportive. The work of Edwards and Alldred (1999) also demonstrates that 'none of the children and young people [in the study] spoke about their parents (mothers) rebuffing their advances and not wishing to be involved in their education' (p.12).

Throughout the questionnaire responses, age emerged as a factor in the extent of parental involvement in the students' schooling. One indication of this is clearly reflected in the questions about choice of school and GCSE subjects. The answers of year 7 and 8 students about choice of school indicate that whilst 28 per cent said that the student made the choice, 24 per cent said their parents made it, and 46 per cent said that it was made by both parents and student. In replying to a question concerning subject choice for GCSE, 57 per cent of year 9 and 10 students said that they chose their subjects themselves, 1 per cent said that their parents did and 39 per cent said that both the student and the parents chose the subjects.

Homework

When they were asked if their parents helped them with their homework, 18 per cent said that they either always did or usually did, and 70 per cent said that they sometimes helped. 12 per cent said that their parents never helped. In most cases parents offered to help at least sometimes and also students felt able to ask for help when they wanted it (see Tables 4, 5, 6 and 7).

Table 4

Do parents help help with homework?	Always (%)	Usually (%)	Sometimes (%)	Never (%)
	6	12	70	12

Table 5

Do parents offer to help with homework?	Always (%)	Usually (%)	Sometimes (%)	Never (%)
	18	18	40	25

Table 6

Do they ask for help?	Always (%)	Usually (%)	Sometimes (%)	Never (%)
	5	11	72	13

Table 7

Do they ask for help?	Always (%)	Usually (%)	Sometimes (%)	Never (%)
Year 7	6	11	77	7
Year 8	7	13	68	12
Year 9	2	10	73	16
Year 10	5	8	68	18

When these responses are examined in relation to year groups parental help is slightly more variable with year 7 students receiving the most help (62 per cent) and year 10 the second most help (50 per cent). This probably reflects the relative insecurity of the year 7 student who is fairly new to the secondary school and the increased demands of GCSE course work on the year 10 student. Parents' offers of help follows the same pattern (59 per cent and 48 per cent respectively). Students' requests for help are more frequent amongst the younger students.

In order to ascertain how they felt about their parents helping them and whether they actually wanted the help or just endured it, the students were asked what they felt about their parents helping or not helping them. Year 7 were the most positive about this and year 10 the least positive (year 7: 76 per cent, year 8: 69 per cent; year 9: 64 per cent and year 10: 57 per cent – either very positive or quite positive). Of those whose parents did not help them (either ever or only at certain times) over 40 per cent didn't mind, or understood why they didn't, with 22 per cent feeling disappointed or worried. The majority of this second group were in years 7 and 8.

The comments from the open questions further illuminate these responses. The younger students said more about how they felt regarding their parents' help. Both girls and boys expressed appreciation, although the girls were slightly more effusive about how it made them feel 'cared about' and that 'it was good to know they [the parents] were there to help'. The boys said that they found it helpful; and it pleased them to have this support. Some referred to the help 'making' it easier' and ensuring that they would not get low marks. A minority of both boys and girls said that they felt guilty about having help and thought that it was like cheating; or that they felt embarrassed or stupid; or that they didn't agree with the advice given.

Year 10 boys were less forthcoming. Most said they appreciated the help but some didn't mind whether their parents helped or not. Some of the boys were pragmatic, saying that it helped them get a better mark and that was what mattered most: it didn't matter who actually helped them. Many of the year 10 girls said that they were 'glad' their parents helped them. Like the younger girls, they found it reassuring and it helped them feel more relaxed about their work and increased their confidence. They also said that it made them see that their parents were interested in them and that they were there if they needed their support. Some said that the help improved their understanding, although others said that sometimes they got confused. Where the parents did not help, year 10 students tended to be either indifferent or else felt they could manage in any case. Some also, like the year 7 and 8 students, said that they felt they should not have help in any case as it was their work and not the responsibility of their parents.

Edwards and Alldred (1999) reported that the young people in their study welcomed parental support not so much for educational reasons but rather because it serves to enhance and develop familial intimacy (p.12). This was borne out by the responses of the younger students but not of the older ones. This I suggest is a further indication of the distancing between this age group and their parents. However, Allatt (1996) also reports that parental concern 'symbolises a place in [their] affections' (p.134) which is regarded as important by all these young people.

The generally positive response from all year groups to parental support indicates the importance for students of having personal support from someone on whom they can rely. Parental involvement with homework was, as far as can be judged from the questionnaire responses, based on negotiation and was optional rather than obligatory.

Homework diaries

The school's requirement for students to complete homework diaries and then get them signed by the parents was a different matter. The homework diary was a means by which school and parent could communicate with each other and also the means by which students were supposed to record their homework. Parents were supposed to sign it once the homework had been completed and then the form tutor was to sign. Students who did not complete it or get the parent to sign it could and often did get a detention.

Over 70 per cent of all respondents said that they completed their homework diaries, either *always* or *usually*, and nearly 80 per cent said that their parents signed them either *always* or *usually*. Whilst substantially more year 7 than year 10 students replied in the affirmative to both of these questions (58 per cent year 7 and 38 per cent year 10 students completed the diaries; of the parents who signed the diaries, 22 per cent were year 7 and 17 per cent year 10) more than half of the year 10 students completed their diaries and over 70 per cent of year 10 parents signed them.

When asked how they felt about having to show their parents the homework diary and get it signed, over half of the students (slightly more of the older ones) expressed indifference. The comments they made explaining their apparent indifference suggest that the homework diary is 'something they have to do', as some of the students remarked. It constitutes a school rule which has to be complied with and which it is out of their power to challenge. The interviews also bore this out. Some of the year 7 students suggested a certain indifference towards the diary amongst the parents as well, as Tom explained: 'My mum hardly looks in it now anyway; she just signs it. She's normally in a rush or something.' And Jenny said, '... they don't look through it, they just sign it anyway. My mum usually signs it because my dad's at work...she just signs it; she wouldn't look through it.'

The views, for those who had them, were a mixture of positive and negative. Once again there were those who expressed the positive aspects of the involvement of their parents, whilst others saw it as an infringement of their independence and autonomous learning autonomy. I will return to this below.

Parents' evenings

The other major area of parental involvement was the parents' evening. This school had one parents' evening a year when the academic and social progress of students was formally reported to the parents. It was also at this event that parents were given the written annual report on their child's progress. 63 per cent of the students said that their parents attended parents' evenings either always or usually and only 11 per cent said that they never did so. Also almost 60 per cent of the students said that they always or usually accompanied their parents to the event.

They were then asked how they felt about going with their parents or not. Those who went with their parents said that they felt this was positive because it gave them an opportunity to hear both the teachers' and their parents' views on their work and progress. Some said it helped to sort out problems. However, even though many of them thought it was a good idea to do so, almost 20 per cent said that they did not like attending the parents' evening. They said that anticipation of what might be said about them made them feel anxious or nervous. Some said it was embarrassing and others said that they dreaded getting told off on the way home.

Those who did not accompany their parents held mixed views about this. Some said they did not mind or did not want to go anyway, but 20 per cent said that they did not feel happy about their parents going without them. They explained that they resented being talked about behind their backs, that they did not like not knowing what was being said and that they did not like being excluded. Some also feared that there must be a problem or something private to discuss or that 'bad comments' would be made.

The year 7 students in the interview responses showed a particular keenness about parents' evening, although they were divided in their views on the merits of accompanying their parents. They all wanted their parents to know what they were doing in school and how they were getting on, as did the year 10 students. However, year 7 students wanted their parents to know everything even if they weren't doing very well, as they felt they would be able to help them improve. The year 10 students, on the other hand were more selective in the information they transmitted, especially if it wasn't very favourable or was concerned with their poor behaviour.

In spite of these views 86 per cent of the students thought parents' evenings were a 'good idea'. Once again they indicated that it gave their parents an opportunity to be involved in their education, to 'get to know what was going on' in school and 'what they [the children] did in school'. Some also said that it gave parents an opportunity to get to know the teachers.

The majority of the students in all year groups seemed to value their parents' help, interest and support. A theme running through their responses was the importance of parents knowing about what they were doing, and how they were achieving. Students were keen that their parents had contact with the school and with their teachers, although they seemed to feel that there was already sufficient contact: when asked if they would like their parents to talk more with the teachers, the majority, 64 per cent , said no, although the year 7 students were almost equally split in their views on this: 48 per cent said yes and 52 per cent said no.

Although it is not possible to judge statistical significance from this base-level analysis of the data, it would seem that the younger students tended towards a greater dependence on their parents' support, and felt more upset if they were not involved, than the older students. This was overwhelmingly the case with the interview responses. This resonates with Connell *et al.*'s (1982) observation that '...the form of attachment to school and the depth of commitment to its programme is subject to change over the years, sometimes to radical mutation' (p.105).

For the older students, control was the key issue. Drawing exclusively on the interview data with the year 10 students I will now explore this aspect more fully.

Parents and students: control or support?

As already discussed, in keeping with the policy of actively seeking im-proved standards, comprehensive schools, at least, are beset with student control strategies and the parents are required to participate in these too. Lowlands School had adopted similar systems to many other comprehensive schools, including Brightside and Acre Lane. The homework diary, the maintenance of which was strongly reinforced, was one such strategy. Getting parents to sign progress reports, and selec-tively posting them to parents, particularly those of students who were not thought to be trustworthy, were others; the system of being put on 'report' for a day or a week was another, together with detentions and exclusions, and the positive reinforcement approach of the prefect and merit systems.

The extent to which students welcomed or tolerated their parents' involvement in, or knowledge about, their schooling depended on how the students saw themselves as learners, or more specifically as achievers. Not surprisingly, the more disaffected students did not want their parents to know about their lack of 'success' or, particularly if they were in any trouble or had failed at a piece of work. However, all students, even those who were less interested in school in general, wanted their parents to know about their successes. Receiving their parents' approbation was very important; not surprisingly it was even more important if they received a reward, which many of the respondents said they did. Related to this was the desire of the students for their parents to feel proud of them: as one boy said, 'You don't bring your son or daughter up to be bad.' He went on to explain that the child doing well reflected positively on the parent and that the parent wanted to hear something positive rather than 'bad stuff all the time'. This is similar to Allatt's (1996) finding that the young people in her study felt also that 'doing your best would make the parents happy' (p.135). Others explained about how telling their parents about their success made them feel good too; Sheila for example said she liked to tell her parents, 'because I'm proud of myself and I want everyone else to be proud of me as well'; and Paula and Clare each said she would tell her parents because 'I get praise.' Others said in relation to this that they liked the attention it gave rise to.

The more successful students tended to feel that the school did not relay sufficient information to their parents when they had done something particularly praiseworthy. Peter explained:

> I think teachers [could] give a more positive feedback because at the moment they [his parents] don't really get anything from my teachers and if we do good work or anything, which is really good, I mean, they don't tell our parents or ring them up [...] which is a bit of a downer.

Most of the students felt that their parents had a right to know how they were getting on at school, at least by receiving the annual progress report.

However, for the most part students were selective about what information they wanted their parents to be given either about 'good' work, or in order to seek support for a homework task, or about other aspects of school. Certain conditions determined whether or not they would confide in their parents, and this usually related to how the event or report reflected on them. Referring to trouble that might arise at school, Sheila explained the conditions which determined whether or not she would confide in her mother:

> I'd tell my mum but only if I think that I hadn't done anything wrong, like if I think the teacher had a go at me for no reason, then I'd tell my mum but if I think I'd done something wrong and the teacher has a go at me then I don't tell my mum.

Some students said that their parents were particularly strict and if they knew they were in trouble in school they would be in more trouble at home; or if they received a poor end-of-year report they would be 'grounded'. As one boy explained, 'I don't want my report to go home because if it's a bad report, I end up getting done or something, my dad will have a go at me or something.' This selective relaying of information or confiding in their parents was, underpinned, it is suggested, by the desire to ensure some control over their own lives. This was most emphatically expressed when they were asked about their futures and what they were going to do after they had taken their GCSEs. We asked the students who should decide this. They all said it was their decision, although most of them also said that they had discussed or would discuss it with their parents. However, where parents held a different view from their child about their futures, the child seemed reluctant to take the parents' advice. One boy, for example, explained, 'They should just advise you what to do but not tell you what to do. They should just, like, give you the information. They've been out in the world and we don't know what's what.' Also friends and personal matters were different, as Christine said: 'Parents can know about homework and stuff but not friends. That's your business not theirs.'

The students who sought their parents' advice about a problem, if they had got into trouble in school or had failed a piece of work and felt concerned about it, were usually those who were successful or quite successful at school. Often this was a way of seeking consolation.

Most of our (year 10) respondents would sometimes request help with their work, if they needed it. Whom they sought this help from mainly depended upon who they thought could actually help them, although teachers were not always, or even nearly always, the first to be asked. (This was also the case with year 7 students). Whether or not they asked a teacher depended on the teacher and whether they felt s/he would be cross with them. Whilst parents may have been willing to help, they were not always in a position to do so, as already discussed. As

Christine said in answer to whether she asked her father for help with homework:

> No I don't because, ... I don't mean to be really horrid, but its moved on since he was at school, like the maths and science, I don't think he really understands it. I think I understand more than he does.

Some of the students said that they talked very little to their parents and in fact hardly saw them in the week, since as soon as they got home from school they went out again, giving their parents hardly time to ask them if they had any homework. For some students, socialising out of the home and after school had taken precedence over school work and socialising in the family. Others had interests and were engaged in activities which took them out of the home too, such as Christine who danced competitively. She actually remarked that she hardly saw her family because of school and her dancing.

Teenage students are growing towards independence; they are actively even if not consciously developing their identities. As Brannen, drawing on Frankenberg (1993), has put it, 'The essence of being a young person is not in being but in becoming...they are adults in the making' (Brannen, 1996, p114); although as Brannen also points out, the notion of 'independence' as individualistic, is problematic since different cultural norms operate. Being shown up for not being able to spell or do maths might not fit well with being a confident, likeable 'jack the lad', as one young person described himself. Being embarrassed or being shown up by their parents was a key concern of the students.

It was essential for students to manage the relationship between the home and the school and to maintain their parents' support, which (as we have seen) most students wanted and valued. But part of this management task, was the need to ensure some level of control for themselves over their own school experience. In order to achieve this most of our respondents recounted examples of avoiding control by parents or school.

Control avoidance – Student control

Connell *et al.* (1982) identified three categories of relations between children and their school: ' resistance, compliance and pragmatism' (p.92). As I have already said, it would seem that more boys more than girls tended to engage in control avoidance. For many of the students, including the more successful ones, there was a degree of indignation about being 'checked up on'. One of the boys, Peter, who had been made a prefect, felt that the homework diary demonstrated a lack of trust on the part of the school. As he explained:

> They [homework diaries] have to be signed once a week [by the tutor] ... it's a feeling of like they don't trust you ...You know, they're doing for your better, well sort of thing – but it's like they don't trust you, so they're checking up on you twice ... I think we do it better if we're left alone to do it instead of someone looking over your shoulder.

Whilst most of the girls accepted the status quo, a minority like Susie resented it, as she said, '[The homework diary's] stupid. I think it's wrong.'

Where a student did not want her or his parents to see a comment, then they just didn't show it to them. Actually keeping parents in ignorance of whether or not they did their homework was fairly easy: as one boy said, 'They [the parents] usually ask me all of the time; I usually say that I've done it or left it at school.' And another boy explained, 'I don't mind [getting the homework diary] signed but if there's something in there that I don't want her [his mum] to see, I try to keep it away.'

Managing the school's control was more difficult since failure to complete homework usually resulted in a detention. This was a punishment the students would accept but did not want their parents to know about. As one boy explained, when given the detention slip he didn't take it home but signed it himself; another said, ' I don't even sign it. I rip it up and then I go to detention.'

Even though most students accepted the importance of parents' evenings, there were times when some students did not want their parents to meet their teachers. One boy, for example, said, 'I don't want to give my mum the letter [about parents' evening] because I don't want her coming up into school and find out what I've been doing.'

With regard to the annual report, although in most cases students wanted their parents to see it, if it was not very good or they felt ashamed of it, then they didn't want to show it to them. The report was given out to the students who saw it first. They were expected to take it home to their parents, who then had to sign a tear-off slip to indicate that they had seen it. It was possible to avoid this monitoring strategy according to one of the students, who had not shown his mother his report. He employed delaying tactics every time his tutor asked him for the slip and in the end it seemed to get forgotten. The students reserved the 'right' to decide whether or not to show their parents the report: as one of the boys said, 'Basically if we want, we can hide it from them. I'd rather show my mum, to show her how I was getting on. If it's well, then she'll probably give me something but again if it's bad, you've got the right to hide it.'

The ultimate control-avoidance strategy is truancy, which Hill and Tisdall (1997) also describe as a form of 'consumer democracy' (p.134); this in turn could be equated with the 'exit' strategy (Hirschman, 1970) which parents too could employ if dissatisfied – even though one is regarded as illegitimate whilst the other isn't. Few of the student respondents, in fact, acknowledged any serial truanting, although a minority said that they had skipped the odd lesson. Most of the students did admit to some kind of control avoidance or control assertion on some occasion; a minority engaged in this frequently and a further minority said that they did not engage in it at all.

Discussion and conclusion

Four key issues can be identified from this analysis:

* Whilst patterns of their views and attitudes did emerge, the students' responses were diverse, marked out by their different circumstances. Policy-makers and many educationalists have been guilty of treating parents as a homogeneous group, and the same criticism can be made about attitudes towards school students. The discernible factors that appear to influence the diversity of student responses include age, gender, social and family circumstances, and academic achievement and ability; we interviewed only one young person from a minority ethnic group and so cannot comment on the impact of ethnicity.

* There is a significant difference between the attitudes of younger students and those of older students in relation to parental involvement. In most cases, students wanted and welcomed their parents'

support; but for the older students this was conditional upon them being able to exert some control over it. The younger students expressed a strong need for their parents' involvement in their schooling: they wanted them to know what they were doing and how well they were doing it.

- Many of the older students objected to certain types of control that they felt the school imposed on them through their parents.

- Many of the older students, but particularly the boys, resisted or avoided certain types of control.

In particular, older students dislike the control imposed upon them even though they endorse their parents' right to know about their progress and seem to welcome the fact that their parents are monitoring their development. However, their objections are concerned with the constraints imposed upon them, which conflict with their own desires.

The level of surveillance described in this chapter is in keeping with the surveillance experienced by parents and teachers too. Julie Allen (1999), in writing about students with special educational needs in mainstream schools, has discussed the issue of surveillance for them. As she says, young people deemed to have 'problems' or who in turn may create 'problems', are more likely to endure a stronger 'gaze' than others. Allen, drawing on Foucault to aid her analysis, discusses the implications of this and argues that the surveillance of the students has an 'individualising effect' which highlights 'difference'; this is then addressed through various assimilationist strategies in order to eradicate the differences (p.21). In my argument presented here, the emphasis is on assimilation: there is seen to be a need for all – parents, students and teachers – to pull together for the same ends; even though of course all students don't end up with the same achievements. The need to 'pull together' underpins the rationale for the monitoring strategies.

There is, then, a sense that the government's educational policies are more concerned with making school students fit in rather than reaching out to and addressing their particular needs. As Reay (1998) has commented, 'students just as their teachers, are a means to an end in the new managerialism' (p.181). It is for this reason that listening to the voices of students is important. So rather than using parents as controllers and monitors of their children's learning, they could be better employed, as can be inferred from the students' responses, working in partnership with their children. Other recent research shows how important school success is for the majority of young people (Flutter *et al.*, 1999), and that young people do have a range of views on their school experience and what they want from it. As I have indicated here, they value the involvement of their parents so long as they have some control over it. There are also indications that certain parent-teacher alliances or encounters at the expense of the child lead to feelings of anxiety. In the study by Kinder *et al.* (1996), which looked at 'disaffected pupils' views' on their educational experience, it was reported that when children felt anxious or frustrated they frequently 'switched off' or reacted negatively. It would be ironic if parental involvement resulted in students' disaffection.

The recent requirements on citizenship education as part of the National Curriculum (DfEE, 1999), together with various pronouncements made by David Blunkett, the Secretary of State for Education, such as the statement quoted in the introduction to this chapter (see also for example Blunkett reported in Cassidy, 1999 and Thornton, 1999), suggest the need to develop amongst school students a sense of participatory democracy and an ability to think critically. Furthermore, the government-initiated discourse on citizenship education seems to be advocating an increased political understanding (in the widest sense), and an understanding of society together with the role of young people within it. The emphasis on parents involvement in their children's schooling in the sense of control, at the expense of the child's own learning autonomy, does not fit easily with this. As Bard (1999) has argued, 'The best way to educate the next generation of citizens in democracy, is to let them act democratically. If students are given a genuine share in responsibility for themselves, they will quickly learn what citizenship means.' Moreover, Edwards and Alldred (1999) have also observed that 'the demand for an increase in parental involvement in schooling renders the children invisible' (p.8).

Clearly students cannot be given the same level of decision-making power about what and how they should learn, as the teachers. As Gutmann (1999) argues 'ceeding them [the students] equal control on all issues would mean denying teachers even a minimal degree of professional autonomy' (p.88). Democratic participation in school nevertheless presents an immense challenge to teachers' own sense of professionalism but it also presents a challenge to the students themselves.

In the next and concluding chapter, the findings of this research study will be reviewed. Implicit within the exploration of the parent-school relationship are the problems but also the possibilities, of this issue of democratic participation for all three groups of key participants: parents, teachers and school students. In the final chapter I will discuss these problems and possibilities.

Notes

1   Some of the questionnaire data used in this chapter and their discussions, are drawn from the article 'Parental Involvement: who wants it?' (Crozier, 1999b) and part of the article is based on a paper that was presented to the British Educational Research Association Annual Conference at the University of Sussex in September 1999.

2   This title has been taken from the publication *Talking Back: pupil views on disaffection* (Kinder *et al.*, 1996).

Chapter 7

Conclusion:
Partners or Protagonists?

I have set out to present aspects of the relationship between parents, and their children's secondary schools, and the various influences upon that relationship. What has emerged are a number of scenarios occupied by parents differentiated by class and gender in relation to teachers. The teachers too are pressured and constrained in their practice by external forces. It has, moreover, been argued that the relationships are played out within a context of control, normalisation and responsibilisation, which affects the key players in different ways.

The declared purposes of parental involvement, as promoted by successive governments and educational researchers, are to improve the educational experience of children and young people, to improve their academic achievements and so to improve their life chances. However, parental involvement as manifested in this study seems to be a long way from achieving this aim equitably. Indeed the outcome of encouraging parents' participation is, as has been seen, to exacerbate the inequalities of access to educational opportunities for mothers and fathers, and in turn their children. This has been partly attributed to the privileged position and advantageous material resources that some parents hold compared with others. As Young (1989) has said, ' In a society where some groups are privileged while others are oppressed... the perspectives and interests of the privileged will tend to dominate... marginalising or silencing those of other groups' (p.257). However, all parent-school relationships, as has been seen, are underpinned by power relations and the struggle, most often implicit rather than explicit, for control or ascendancy. This takes place through the teachers rather than between the parents themselves, and as discussed in Chapters 3, 4 and 5, teachers were aware of the impact powerful parents can have on the rights or 'voice' of less powerful parents, as well as on themselves.

Parental involvement and school choice are policy initiatives pur-portedly designed to create opportunities for parents to participate in and support the achievement of their children. Failure to take advantage of this, or even worse failure to behave 'responsibly', is therefore deemed to be the fault of the parent – most likely the mother. Working-class parents were frequently perceived in this way by the teachers. 'Un-motivated' children, for example, were associated with 'unmotivated' parents, and 'unmotivated' parents were working-class; there was no question that anything could be amiss with the school experience itself. As recounted earlier, the Secretary of State for Education, David Blunkett, also seemingly holds (certain kinds of) mothers responsible for the education, or lack of education, of their children, just as Walker-dine and Lucey remind us that Douglas in his seminal study (1964) held 'working-class mothers responsible for the success or failure of the new post-war equal opportunities' (Walkerdine and Lucey, 1989, p.1).

The terms upon which parental participation are based are determined by the school and the policy agenda. With respect to the latter, it is only through the school governing body that parents have a potential say in policy and curricular related decision-making, and although there are now an increased number of parents on these bodies, they do not have a mandate. Whether having a mandate in itself would be a good thing is also debatable (see for example Phillips, 1993), especially as it is again the most articulate, educated and knowledgeable parents who are best placed to take up these roles and these parents are not always repre-sentative of the diversity of needs and viewpoints. However, even though there are an increased number of parent governors, there is still a lack of formal mechanisms for parental participation in schools (Hatcher, 1999). The point here is that parental participation is super-ficial, irrespective of social class. There are, nevertheless, different implications of this for middle-class and working-class parents, as Hatcher (1999) has also commented. As demonstrated in this study, middle-class parents are more able to compensate for the lack of such mechanisms and lack of knowledge through their access to social and cultural capital and social networks.

Parental involvement is also underpinned by control and regulation of parents' behaviour as represented by the Home-School Agreements

Policy (DfEE, 1998a and implemented in September 1999) and the Homework Policy (DfEE, 1998b and implemented in September, 1999). Commenting on homework, Ulich (1989) has pointed out that 'Through homework the school's standards and expectations are brought directly into the family, parents... are confronted with demands for support...' (p.182 cited in Ribbens, 1993). Walkerdine and Lucey again, writing ten years ago, express a view which continues to have resonance today:

> Women's labour, in the form of mothering, is an essential part of a story about class and social democracy in Britain, in which the regulation of women became seen as central, so great was the threat posed by the possibility that women would not properly mother. (1989, p2)

The parenting classes and the literacy and numeracy classes for mothers (*sic*) (referred to in Chapter 1) are part of the same strategy. Parents' role in this is thus not only about overseeing and monitoring school work but also about contributing to their child's education in the home and family set-up. This is described by Edwards and Alldred (1998) as the incorporation of 'familialisation' into 'institutionalisation' for both children and their mothers. It is the blurring of the old boundaries between the public and the private which 'no longer shield us' (Beck, 1997, p.12).

Given the increased demands upon parents' time to fulfil these new obligations of monitoring, it is not surprising that they have little time to spend attending additional meetings and events. As was shown in Chapter 4, mothers in particular explained that work, childcare commitments, lack of transport and so on, all served to constrain their involvement with the secondary school once their child was there.

The processes involved in the 'institutionalisation' of family practices, as has been seen, find more fertile ground in middle-class homes, where there is a greater interconnectedness between home and school. Nevertheless, whilst parental/mothers' involvement increases the burden particularly on and lone mothers (David, 1998), Walkerdine and Lucey (1989) remind us of the oppression experienced by middle- class mothers too, in the way that they are compelled to utilise every moment for pedagogical purposes, having internalised the government's project with its emphasis on driving up standards, fast- tracking and competing to see 'who can get there first'. This receptivity by middle-class parents places both the mothers (essentially) and the children on a pedagogic treadmill (Walkerdine and Lucey, 1989).

For working-class parents driven by their resolve to maintain a separation between home and school, the boundary is less permeable, even though boundary maintenance and boundary management exist, to a greater or lesser extent, for all the key actors here. Whilst it has been argued throughout this book that there is no single explanation for the nature of the relationship between working-class or middle-class parents and the teachers of their children, it has also been argued that parents display a resistance to normalisation and assimilation. As has been said in Chapter 4, this is not in relation to a rejection of education per se but rather it is a stand against being placed in a position of rejection or of feeling vulnerable or being humiliated. Those working- class parents who did attend meetings such as the Parents' Forum at Acre Lane frequently reported that they did not understand what was being discussed and thus felt excluded. Other parents described similar events as, for example, 'not for us', echoing this demarcation; and there were the parents who described attendance at these meetings as being dependent on whether, in the words of Mrs Foster (Brightside), 'you're either in or you're way on the outside and I always thought myself way on the outside'. Such resistance is also a stand against being incorporated into a form of behaviour which they considered unacceptable: the only way such a parent might have been accepted would have been to have become 'a pushy parent', someone who 'is up there all of the time', and that was not how they wanted to be.

Some parents did describe attempting to intervene on academic matters on their children's behalf, like Mrs Horn (Chapter 3), who reluctantly questioned a teacher about an aspect of the science curriculum and did so only because her daughter asked her to. She felt she was given short shrift by being told, 'That's the way it's done'. She felt powerless but also affronted by the response (Crozier, 1999a). Other parents, such as Mrs McClelland in Chapter 4, explained that there was little point in questioning or putting their point of view because the teachers' view prevailed.

Working-class parents stepping back from this situation and maintaining a separation between home and school can be likened, in some ways, as alluded to in Chapter 4, to Willis's lads (Willis, 1977) in the sense that 'they are refusing to collude in their own suppression' (p.128). They can see (as the lads could see about education) that this type of involvement was not for the likes of them. Parents' rejection of parental involvement as designated by the school can be seen as a form of 'penetration' into the process of normalisation and assimilation. Of course in taking this stance, just like the lads, the parents give up any claims to wrest control, or power from the teachers or to position themselves in equal relations with the them (Willis, 1977 pp.109-110). However, as Willis also points out, working-class engagement with the educational status quo only results at the very best, in most cases, in the achievement of low-level qualifications, which have little bearing on job choice; as such this capitulation merely serves to legitimate the class structure. If I may continue with this comparison, were working-class parents to engage with the process of normalisation, they too could be said to be colluding with its perpetuation, and this would have a discriminatory effect upon them as a class group.

Another theme that pervades parent-teacher relationships is that of trust. Teachers, as we saw in Chapter 5, spoke frequently of wanting parents to trust them: to let them get on with the job and leave it to the professionals. Giddens (1991) explains trust as 'a form of 'faith' in which confidence vested in probable outcomes expresses a commitment to something rather than just cognitive understanding' (p.27). He goes on to elaborate, suggesting that trust is 'related to absence in time and in space' or that trust is required when we cannot see what is going on and that ' the prime condition of requirements of trust are not lack of power but lack of full information' (p.33). Middle-class parents' lack of trust in the teachers, as perceived by the teachers, and as demonstrated by their questioning of teachers, may be understood in this way; that is, through their own acquired knowledge they have less need or desire to 'trust', or rely on, the professional. Middle-class parents are socially and culturally positioned in such a way that they have always had access to educational knowledge and experience. Even now, with the constant changes in educational systems and organisation, and in curricular and assessment requirements, they are able to reappropriate such knowledge and become reskilled (Giddens, 1991), which allows them to continue to make informed choices and decisions but which also ensures that they operate most often on an individual basis (Vincent, 2000), as in fact the marketisation of education encourages.

The notion of individualisation however, according to Beck (1994), is not based on 'the free decision of individuals' (p.14), but given the conditions of the market, as in the sphere of education, or in a post-modern or post-traditional context, people are compelled to operate in individualistic ways. They are enabled to recreate themselves, to redefine their identity, but implicit in all this is the willingness and need to act: an expectation of action, of taking responsibility.

In later work Giddens (1994) develops further his thesis on trust shifting his position from 'trust in expert systems' to the development of active trust. Lash (1994), commenting on this, explains, 'Active trust emerges when institutions become reflexive and the propositions of the experts are opened up for critique and contestation. With such critical activity of the lay public, trust in expert systems becomes not passive but active' (p.202). This is exactly the nature of the actions of middle-class parents, who in turn are seen as taking on the requirement of responsibilisation. But paradoxically they are regarded from the teachers' perspective as a challenge and even a threat.

Ironically (in the light of teachers' criticisms of these parents), working-class parents do indeed trust the teachers, in that they rely on them and leave them to do their job. Postmodern developments (such as the marketisation of education, and the new managerialism) have done little to empower working-class parents in their involvement with schools. They have little choice but to trust in the professionals: as they have been quoted as saying, the teachers have been trained to teach but they have not. Again according to Giddens (1991), trust is balanced against risk – a level of acceptable risk: in trusting teachers, working-class parents demonstrate their willingness to take this degree of risk. However, deciding whether they want to diminish the boundary between home and school or to maintain it is much more within their control; to allow the school to enter their home and family life is a risk they were not prepared to take.

Parent-teacher relationships are not therefore a given but are characterised by a struggle for control and definition. From their own perspective, teachers are seeking to assert control and maintain it in their interactions with parents. As we have seen, they have two broad sets of relationships to manage: with the assertive, demanding middle-class parents on the one hand, and with the seemingly passive, disengaged working-class parents on the other. In order to maintain their control, they need to establish, for the former, and maintain, for the latter, an image of professional expertise. Following Giddens (1991), who draws on Goffman's concepts of 'front and backstage performances', I have shown in Chapter 5 how teachers concealed some of what they do. This was demonstrated by the keystage 4 head of year, who did not reveal to the irate parents how he dealt with the offending teacher; in fact he did not admit to the offence as such at all. A key element of this behaviour, as Giddens points out, is the belief that lay people will feel more confident in the professionals if they are not able to observe the 'mistakes' they make.

The parents' evening serves the precise purpose of allowing teachers to display their expertise in a controlled manner. In Giddens' (1991) terms, the parents' evening serves to 'reembed the social relations' between the teachers and the parents; as Giddens explains, 'reembedding represents a means of anchoring trust in the trustworthiness and integrity' (p. 87), in this case of teachers. Teachers talked about how they had to present themselves in the best light; to show parents that they knew what they were about; knew their subject, and knew the children (see Chapter 5). Parents' evenings are part of the process of managing parent-school relations; they provide further opportunity to tie parents into 'trust relations' (Giddens, 1991) and to assure parents that their children are in 'good hands'. Parents' evenings thus provide a veneer of professional competence and harmonious relations between students, teachers and parents.

Some parents did indicate that they saw through the charade but nevertheless they were willing to go along with it. It is after all an opportunity for parents too to display their trustworthiness as 'responsible involved parents'.

This brings me to the school students who tend to be sidelined in this relationship and yet are pivotal to it. For the younger students who we interviewed there was no issue here. They wanted their parents' support and involvement and overall they felt they had this adequately. For the older students the key issue was the need to establish some control over parents' involvement and to play a greater part in the parent-school relationship. Their struggle to achieve this is bound up in the everyday struggle for survival in school but it is also implicitly part of the struggle for a more participatory partnership between all key players.

And so what of parent-school relationships, is it a partnership or is it a contest for domination of one by the other? I have argued that it is a contest between the two broad groups of parents and the teachers. Between the middle-class parents and the teachers it is a contest that is more equally balanced, although in this study the middle-class parents often had the upper hand. The contest between the working-class parents and the teachers, however, has been seen to be unequal, with the working-class parents being aware of this and thus, frequently, opting out.

Whitty *et al.* (1998) point out that the dismantling of bureaucratic control of education provision in Britain (and the four other countries that they looked at) has significant consequences for school-parent relationships; but they also question the impact on educational opportunities in the search to alleviate inequalities of access and participation, and in fact conclude that in many cases these may have been exacerbated (p.126). To assess the desirability of parental involvement it is necessary to take into account the consideration that without the participation of all key players, then change for disadvantaged and disempowered groups is unlikely to happen. Carnoy (1983) has argued the need for grass roots struggle in this way:

> Democracy has been developed by social movements and those intellectuals and educators who were able to implement democratic reforms in education did so in part through appeals to such movements. If the working people, minorities and women who have formed social movements pressing for greater democracy in our society cannot be mobilized behind equality in education.... there is absolutely no possibility that equality in education will be implemented (pp. 401-2)

Of course as Giroux (1989) has argued: 'Democracy is a site of struggle and as a social practice, is informed by competing ideological conceptions of power, politics and community' (pp.28-29) Participatory democracy as part of that, needs to face up to the demands and challenges posed by diverse groups. It needs to address the politics of difference; it needs to provide a space for 'those unique voices and social practices [which] contain their own principles and validity while sharing in a public consciousness and discourse' (p.31). This, of course, is more easily said than done. Yeatman (1994) has highlighted the potential of democratic participation through social movements, or as Martin and Vincent (1999) describe them, 'little polities'; and Martin and Vincent have begun to explore their existence in Britain, identifying the problems but also the possibilities of such groupings.

At a very basic level, within school, parental involvement that is based upon understandings of participatory democracy can only be brought about if mutual trust and respect is established. This will require parents trusting the teachers but likewise teachers trusting the parents. For all concerned it will incur a level of risk. With respect to working-class parents, before any trust can be placed, there will be the need to challenge to the negative attitudes, negative stereotyping and, albeit unintentional discriminatory practices levelled against them. Linked to this is the need to address cultural diversity and the politics of difference. There has been much discussion of how democracies can deliver on equality while accommodating and welcoming difference (to paraphrase Phillips, 1993) but only limited answers. As Whitty *et al.* (1998) have said, whilst spaces for debate and for minority voices to be heard may open up from time to time, 'there is nothing to indicate that the strength of the state has been substantially reduced...its willingness and capacity for internal regulation would appear to have remained... undiminished' (p.137). Moreover, as Walkerdine and Lucey (1989) point out arguing for 'equal but different' and recognising cultural pluralism is fatuous if exploitation and oppression is ignored. This would seem to be the major challenge and cannot be underestimated; in the light of this, the control of parents and students, normalisation, and monitoring strategies as a basis for parental involvement need to be reappraised.

References

Adler, M., Petch, A. and Tweedie, J. (1989) *Parental Choice and Educational Policy.* Edinburgh: Edinburgh University Press

Aldous, J. (1978) *Family Careers: developmental change in families.* London: John Wiley

Allatt, P. (1996) 'Conceptualizing Parenting from the Standpoint of Children: relationship and transition in the life course' in J. Brannen and M. O'Brien (eds) *Children in Families, Research and Policy.* London: Falmer

Allen, J. (1999) *Actively Seeking Inclusion.* London: Falmer

Anderson, E.M. and Clarke, L. (1982) *Disability in Adolescence.* London: Methuen

Apple, M.W. (1988) *Teachers and Texts: A political economy of class and gender relations in education.* London: Routledge

Apple, M.W. (1995) (second edition) *Education and Power.* London: Routledge

Atkin, J. and Bastiani, J. (1988a) *Listening to Parents.* London: Croom Helm

Atkin, J. and Bastiani, J. (1988b) 'Training Teachers to Work with Parents', in J. Bastiani (ed.) *Parents and Teachers 2; From policy to practice.* Slough: NFER-Nelson

Ball, S.J. (1990) 'Management as Moral Technology: a Luddite analysis', in S. Ball (ed.) *Foucault and Education, Disciplines and Knowledge.* London: Routledge

Ball, S.J. (1993) 'Education Policy, Power Relations and Teachers' Work'. *British Journal of Educational Studies* 41: 2 pp.106-21

Ball, S. J. (1994) *Education Reform.* Buckingham: Open University Press

Ball, S. J. and Vincent, C. (1998) 'I heard it on the grapevine': 'hot' knowledge and school choice'. *British Journal of Sociology of Education* 19: 3 pp.377-400

Bastiani, J. (1989) *Working With Parents: a whole school approach.* Slough: NFER-Nelson

Barber, M. (1996) *The Learning Game.* London: Victor Gollancz

Bard, J. (1999) 'Students Need Real Power'. *Times Educational Supplement.* 4th June

Barnard, N. (1999) 'The Challenge of Confrontational Parents'. *Times Educational Supplement.* 23 April

Beck, U. (1994) 'The Reinvention of Politics: towards a theory of reflexive modernization', in U. Beck, A. Giddens and S. Lash *Reflexive Modernization: politics, tradition and aesthetics in the modern social order.* Cambridge: Polity Press

Beck, U. (1997) *Reinventing Politics.* Cambridge: Polity Press

Beresford, E. and Hardie, A. (1996) 'Parents and Secondary Schools: a different approach?', in J. Bastiani and S. Wolfendale (eds) *Home-School Work in Britain: review, reflection and development.* London: David Fulton

Birenbaum-Carmeli, D. (1999) Parents Who Get What They Want: on empowerment of the powerful'. *The Sociological Review* 47: 1 pp.62-90

Blyth, E. and Milner, J. (1994) 'Exclusion from School and Victim Blaming'. *Oxford Review of Education* 20: 3 pp.293-306

Bourdieu, P. (1984) *Distinction: a social critique of the judgement of taste.* London: Routledge

Bourdieu, P. and Passeron, J. C. (1977) *Reproduction in Education, Society and Culture.* London: Sage

Bourdieu, P., Passeron, J. C. and De Saint Martin, M. (1994) *Academic Discourse.* Cambridge: Polity Press

Bowe, R. and Ball, S. with Gold, A. (1992) *Reforming Education and Changing Schools: case studies in policy sociology.* London: Routledge

Brannen, J. (1996) 'Discourses of Adolescence: young people's independence and autonomy within families', in J. Brannen and M. O'Brien (eds) *Children in Families, Research and Policy.* London: Falmer

Brannen, J., Moss, P., Owen, C. and Wale, C. (1997) 'Mothers, Fathers and Employment: parents and the labour market 1984-1994'. *DfEE Research Report 10*

Brannen, J. and Moss, P. (1998) 'The Polarisation and Intensification of Parental Employment in Britain: consequences for children, family and community'. *Community, Work and Family* 1: 3 pp.229-47

Brown, P. (1987) *Schooling Ordinary Kids, Inequality: unemployment and the new vocationalism.* London: Tavistock

 Brown, P. (1997) 'The 'Third Wave': Education and the Ideology of Parentocracy', in A. H. Halsey, H. Lauder, P. Brown and A. Stuart Wells, (eds) *Education: culture, economy, society.* Oxford: Oxford University Press

Buchanan, C. M., Maccoby, E.E. and Dornbusch, S. M. (1991) 'Caught between Parents: adolescents' experience in divorced homes'. *Child Development* 62 pp.1008-29

Bullock, A. and Thomas, H. (1997) *Schools at the Centre? a study of decentralization.* London: Routledge

Callaghan, J. (1976) 'Towards a National Debate'. *Education* 148: 17

Carnoy, M. (1983) 'Education, Democracy and Social Conflict'. *Harvard Educational Review* 53: 4 pp.401-2

Carvel, J. (1998) 'Labour Targets Lazy Parents'. *Guardian* 16 January

Cassidy, S. (1999) 'Blunkett Plays Identity Card'. *Times Educational Supplement.* 28 May

Chubb, J. E. and Moe, T. M. (1997) 'Politics, Markets and the Organization of Schools', in A.H. Halsey, H. Lauder, P. Brown and A. Stuart Wells (eds) *Education: culture, economy and society.* Oxford: Oxford University Press

Clarke, A. and Power, S. (1998) *Could Do Better. School Reports and Parents' Evenings, a study of secondary school practice.* London: Research and Information on State and Education Trust

Codd, J (1993) 'Governance, Leadership and Accountability in New Zealand Schools'. Paper presented at the Annual Conference of the British Educational Research Association. Liverpool, 10-13 September 1993

Coldron, J. and Boulton, P. (1991) "Happiness' as a criterion of parents' choice of school'. *Journal of Education Policy* 6: 2 pp.169-78

Coleman, J. (1998) 'Social Capital in the Creation of Human Capital', in A.H. Halsey, H. Lauder, P. Brown and A. Stuart Wells (eds) *Education: culture, economy and society.* Oxford: Oxford University Press

Connell, R. Ashenden, D.J. Kessler, S. and Dowsett, G.W. (1982) *Making the Difference: schools, families and social division.* London: Allen and Unwin

Crozier, G. (1996) 'Competing Discourses in the Implementation of Anti-Racist Education'. Paper presented at the European Conference on Educational Research. Seville, 12-15 September

Crozier, G. (1997) 'Empowering the Powerful'. *British Journal of Sociology of Education* 18: 2, pp.187-200

Crozier, G. (1998) 'Parents and Schools: partnership or surveillance?' *Journal of Educational Policy* 13: 1 pp.125-136

Crozier, G. (1999a) 'Is It a Case of 'We Know When We're Not Wanted?': the parents' perception of parent-teacher roles and relationships'. *Educational Research* 41: 3 pp.315-28

Crozier, G. (1999b) 'Parental Involvement: who wants it?' *International Studies in Sociology of Education* 9: 2 pp.111-30

Dandeker, C. (1990) *Surveillance, Power and Modernity.* Cambridge: Polity Press

David, M. E. (1993a) *Parents Education and Gender Reform.* Cambridge: Polity Press

David, M. (1993b) 'Home-School Relations', in M. David, R. Edwards, M. Hughes and J. Ribbens, *Mothers and Education: Inside Out? Exploring family-education policy and experience.* London: Macmillan

David, M., Edwards, R., Hughes, M. and Ribbens, J. (1993) *Mothers and Education: Inside Out? Exploring family-education policy and experience.* London: Macmillan

David, M., West, A. and Ribbens, J. (1994) *Mothers' Intuition: choosing secondary schools.* London: Falmer

David, M., Edwards, R. and Alldred, P. (1998) 'Children's understandings of parental involvement in education'. *Economic and Social Research Council Award No L129251012*

David, M. E. (1998) *The Fragmenting Family: does it matter?* London: IEA Health and Welfare Unit

David, M. (1999) 'Home, Work, Families and Children: New Labour, new directions and new dilemmas'. *International Studies in Sociology of Education,* 9: 3 pp.209-29

Davies, J. (1993) *The Family: is it just another life-style choice?* London: IEA, Health and Welfare Unit

Deem, R., Brehony. K. and Heath, S., (1995) *Active Citizenship and the Governing of Schools.* Buckingham: Open University Press

DfE (1992) *Choice and Diversity.* London: HMSO

DfEE (1997a) *Excellence in Schools.* London: HMSO

DfEE (1997b) *Circular 2/97 Reports on Pupil Achievements in Secondary Schools in 1996/1997.* London: DfEE

DfEE (1998a) *Draft Guidance on Home-School Agreements.* London: DfEE Publications Centre

DfEE (1998b) *Homework Guidelines For Primary/Secondary Schools, Draft Consultation.* London: DfEE

DfEE (1998c) *Teachers, Meeting the Challenge of Change.* Green Paper. London: DfEE Publications CM4164

DfEE (1999) *Citizenship Will Allow Children to Make a Real Difference* www.dfee.gov.uk/news/319.htm

Donzelot, J. (1979) *The Policing of Families.* London: Hutchinson

Douglas, J.W.B. (1964) *The Home and the School.* Glasgow: McGibbon and Kee

Duncan, S. and Edwards, R. (1998) *Single Mothers in an International Context.* London: UCL Press

Edwards, R. and Alldred, P. (1998) 'Bodily Location in Home-School Relations: children's understandings'. Paper presented at the British Sociological Association Annual Conference. University of Edinburgh, 6-9 April

Edwards, R. and Alldred, P. (1999) 'Home-School Relations: children and young people negotiating familialisation, institutionalisation and individualisation'. Paper presented at the British Educational Research Association Annual Conference. University of Sussex 2-5 September

Edwards, R. and David, M. (1997) 'Where Are the Children in Home-School Relations? notes towards a research agenda'. *Children and Society* 11 pp.194-200

Evans, J. and Vincent, C. (1995) 'Constraints on Choice: parental choice and special education'. Paper presented at the ESRC/CEPAM Invitation Seminar: Research on Parental Choice and School Response: emerging implications for policy and future studies. Milton Keynes, 7-8 June

Everard, K.B. and Morris, G. (1996) *Effective School Management.* Third edition. London: Paul Chapman

Featherstone, M. (1991) *Consumer Culture and Postmodernism.* London: Sage

Fine, M. (1997) 'Apparent Involvement: Reflections on Parents, Power and Urban Public Schools', in A. H. Halsey, H. Lauder, P. Brown, and A. Stuart Wells, (eds) *Education: culture, economy, society.* Oxford: Oxford University Press

Finch, J. and Mason, J. (1993) *Negotiating Family Responsibilities.* London: Routledge

Flutter, J., Ruddock, J., Adams, H. Johnson, M. and Maden, M. (1999) *Improving Learning: the pupils' agenda – secondary schools.* Cambridge: Homerton College

Foucault, M. (1977) *Discipline and Punish: the birth of the prison.* London: Penguin

Frankenberg, R. (1993) 'Trust, Culture, Language and Time', Consent Conference Number 2, Young People's Psychiatric treatment and Consent. London Institute of Education, Social Science Research Unit

Gamarnikow, E. and Green, A. (1999) 'Developing Social Capital: dilemmas, possibilities and limitations in education', in A. Hayton (ed.) *Tackling Disaffection and Social Exclusion*. London: Kogan Page

Gewirtz, S., Ball, S. and Bowe, R. (1995) *Markets, Choice and Equity*. Buckingham: Open University Press

Gewirtz, S. (1997) 'The Education Market: labour relations in schools and teacher unionism in the UK', in R. Glatter, P. Woods, C. Bagley (eds) *Choice and Diversity in Schooling*. London: Routledge

Giddens, A. (1984) *The Constitution and Society*. Cambridge: Polity Press

Giddens, A. (1991) *The Consequences of Modernity*. Cambridge: Polity Press

Giddens, A. (1994) *Beyond Left and Right*. Cambridge: Polity Press

Giddens, A. (1998) *The Third Way: the renewal of social democracy*. Cambridge: Polity Press

Giroux, H. (1989) *Schooling for Democracy*. London: Routledge

Giroux, H. (1992) *Border Crossings*. London: Routledge

Giroux, H. (1997) *Pedagogy and the Politics of Hope*. Oxford: Westview Press

Glaser, B. and Strauss, A. (1967) *The Discovery of Grounded Theory*. Chicago: Aldine

Glatter, R. Woods, P. A. and Bagley, C. (1997) 'Diversity, Differentiation and Hierarchy: school choice and parental preference', in R. Glatter, P.A. Woods, and C. Bagley (eds) *Choice and Diversity in Schooling: perspectives and prospects*. London: Routledge

Goacher, B. and Reid, M. I. (1985) *School Reports to Parents: a study of policy and practice in secondary school*. Slough: NFER-Nelson

Goldthorpe, J. and Hope, K. (1978) *The Social Grading of Occupations*. Oxford: Oxford University Press

Goldthorpe, J. (1987) *Social Mobility and Class Structure in Modern Britain*. Second edition. Oxford: Clarendon Press

Grace, G. (1995) *School Leadership: beyond educational management. An essay in policy scholarship*. London: Falmer

Gutmann, A. (1999) *Democratic Education*. Revised edition. New Jersey, USA: Princeton University Press

Hargreaves, A. (1994) *Changing Teachers, Changing Times: teachers' work and culture in the postmodern age*. London: Cassell

Harris, C. (1983) *The Family and Industrial Society*. London: Allen and Unwin

Harris, D. (1987) *Justifying State Welfare: the New Right vs the Old Left*. Oxford: Basil Blackwell

Hatcher, R. (1999) 'Exclusion, Consultation or Empowerment?' *Education and Social Justice* 2:1 pp.45-57

Hatton, E. (1985) 'Equality, Class and Power: a case study'. *British Journal of Sociology of Education*, 6: 3, pp.273-92

Hill, M. and Tisdall, K. (1997) *Children and Society*. London: Addison Wesley, Longman

Hirschman, A. O. (1970) *Exit, Voice and Loyalty*. Cambridge, Massachusetts: Harvard University Press

Hoy, W. K. and Miskel C. G. (1989) 'Schools and their External Enviroments', in R.Glatter (ed.) *Educational Institutions and Their Environments: managing the boundaries*. Buckingham: Open University Press.

Hoyle, E. and John, P.D. (1995) *Professional Knowledge and Professional Practice*. London: Cassell

Home Office (1997a) *Crime and Disorder Bill*. London: The Stationery Office

Home Office (1997b) *No More Excuses: A new approach to tackling youth crime in England and Wales*. London: The Stationery Office

Hughes, M., Wikeley, F. and Nash, T. (1994) *Parents and Their Children's Schools*. Oxford: Blackwell

Hughes, M. (1997) 'The National Curriculum in England and Wales: a lesson in externally imposed reform?' *Educational Administration Quarterly* 33: 2 pp.183-97

Hutton, W. (1995) *The State We're In*. London: Jonathan Cape

Jacob, E. and Jordan, C. (1993) 'Understanding Minority Education: framing the issues', in E. Jacob and C. Jordan (eds) *Minority Education: anthropological perspectives*. Norwood, New Jersey: Ablex

Jagger, G. and Wright, C. (1999) 'Introduction: changing family values', in G. Jagger and C. Wright (eds) *Changing Family Values*. London and New York: Routledge

Jeffs, T. (1995) 'Children's Educational Rights in a New ERA?' in B. Franklin (ed.) *The Handbook of Children's Rights*. London: Routledge

Johnson, D. and Ransom, J (1988) 'Family and School: the relationship re-assessed', in J. Bastiani (ed.) *Parents and Teachers Part 2*. Slough: NFER-Nelson

Jonathan, R. (1990) State Education Service or Prisoner's Dilemma: the 'hidden hand' as source of education policy. *British Journal of Educational Studies* 38: 2 pp.116-32

Jowett, S. and Baginsky, M. (1991) *Building Bridges*. Slough: NFER-Nelson.

Kickert, W. (1991) 'Steering at a Distance: a new paradigm of public governance in Dutch higher education'. Paper presented at the European Consortium for Political Research. University of Essex, March

Kinder, K.,Wakefield, A. and Wilkin, A. (1996) *Talking Back: pupils' views on disaffection*. Slough: NFER-Nelson

Kinder, K., Wilkin, A. and Wakefield, A. (1997) *Exclusion, Who Needs It?* Slough: NFER-Nelson

Kyriacou, C. (1987) 'Teacher Stress and Burnout: an international review'. *Educational Research* 29, pp.1146-52

Labov, W. (1969) 'The Logic of Non-Standard English', in P.P. Giglioli (ed.) *Language and Social Context.* Harmondsworth: Penguin

Lareau, A. (1989) *Home Advantage.* London: Falmer

Lareau, A. (1997) 'Social Class, Differences in Family-School Relationships: the importance of cultural capital' in A.H. Halsey, H. Lauder, P. Brown and A. Stuart Wells (eds) *Education: culture, economy and society.* Oxford: Oxford University Press

Lash, S. (1994) 'Reflexivity and Its Doubles: structure, aesthetics, community', in U. Beck, A. Giddens, S. Lash (eds) *Reflexive Modernization: politics, tradition and aesthetics in the modern social order.* Cambridge: Polity Press

Lawn, M. and Ozga, J. (1988) 'The Educational Worker? A reassessment of teachers', in J. Ozga (ed.) *Schoolwork: approaches to the labour process of teaching.* Buckingham: Open University Press

Leithwood, K., Menzies, T., Jantzi. D. and Leithwood, J. (1996) 'School Restructuring: transformational leadership and amelioration of teacher burnout'. *Anxiety, Stress and Coping: an International Journal* 9, pp.199-215

Le Grand, J. and Bartlett, W. (1993) *Quasi Markets and Social Policy.* London: Macmillan

Le Grand, J. (1996) 'Knights, Knaves or Pawns? human behaviour and social policy'. Unpublished paper. School of Policy Studies, University of Bristol

Levačić, R. (1995) *Local Management of Schools: analysis and practice.* Buckingham: Open University Press

Lister, R. (1996) 'Back to the Family: family policies and politics under the Major government', in H. Jones and J. Millar (eds) *The Politics of the Family.* Aldershot: Avebury

Lowe, R. (1993) *The Welfare State in Britain since 1945.* London: Macmillan

Macbeth, A. (1989) *Involving Parents: effective parent-teacher relations.* Oxford: Heinemann

Maclure, M. and Walker, B. (1999) Secondary School Parents' Evenings. End of Award report to the Economic Social Research Council. Award number: R000222287. University of East Anglia, Centre for Applied Research in Education

Maclachlan, K. (1996) 'Good Mothers Are Women Too: the gender implications of parental involvement in education', in J. Bastiani and S. Wolfendale (eds) *Home-School Work in Britain: review, reflection and development.* London: David Fulton

Macleod, D. (1996) 'Would you sign this?' *Education Guardian.* 15 October

Mahoney, P. and Moos, L. (1998) 'Democracy and School Leadership in England and Denmark'. *British Journal of Educational Studies* 46: 3 pp.302-17

Martin, J. (1999) 'Social Justice, Education Policy and the Role of Parents: a question of choice or voice? *Education and Social Justice* 1: 2, pp.48-61

Martin, J. and Vincent, C. (1999) 'Parental Voice: an exploration' Paper presented at the Interrnational Sociology of Education Conference, Sheffield, January

McClelland, R., Thomas, G., Vass, P. and Webb, J. (1995) *Parent Choice: a survey of 659 parents.* Oxford: Oxford Brookes University, School of Education

McCormick, R. (1982) 'School-Based Accounting: communication with parents', in R. McCormick (ed.) *Calling Education to Account.* Milton Keynes: Open University Press

McKibbin, C., Cooper, T.J., Blanche, J., Douglas, P., Granzen, J. and Greer-Richardson, B. (1998) 'Bridges and Broken Finger Nails', in B. Atweh, S. Kemmis and P. Weeks (eds) *Action Research in Practice.* London: Routledge

Meighan, R. and Siraj-Blatchford, I. (1997) *A Sociology of Educating.* Third edition. London: Cassell

Merttens, R. and Vass, J. (1993) *Partnership in Maths: parents and schools.* London: The Falmer Press

Merttens, R and Newland, A. (1996) 'Home Works: shared maths and shared writing', in J. Bastiani and S. Wolfendale (eds) *Home-School Work in Britain.* London: David Fulton

Morgan. I. (1989) 'The Politics of Parental Involvement', in F. Macleod (ed.) *Parents and Schools: the contemporary challenge.* London: Falmer

OFSTED (1995) *Reporting Pupils' Achievements.* London: HMSO

Ozga, J. (2000) *Policy Research in Educational Settings.* Buckingham and Philadelphia: Open University Press

Phillips, A. (1991) *Engendering Democracy.* Cambridge: Polity Press

Phillips, A. (1993) *Democracy and Difference.* Philadelphia, Pennsylvania: Pennsylvania State University

Plowden Report (1967) *Children and Their Primary Schools. Central Advisory Council for Education.* London: HMSO

Pollard, A. (1985) *The Social World of the Primary School.* London: Cassell

Prestage, M. (1994) 'Volunteers 'default' on duties'. *Times Educational Supplement,* 12 August

Pugh, G., (1989) 'Parents and Professionals in Pre-School Services: is partnership possible?' in S. Wolfendale, (ed.) *Parental Involvement: developing networks between home, school and community.* London: Cassell

QCA/DfEE (1997) *Assessment and Reporting Arrangements 1998: Key Stage 3.* London: HMSO

Reay, D. (1998) *Class Work: mothers' involvement in their children's primary schooling.* London: UCL Ltd

Ribbens, J. (1990) *Accounting for Our Children: differing perspectives on 'family life' in middle income households.* Unpublished PhD , CNAA, South Bank Polytechnic

Ribbens, J. (1993) 'Having a Word with the Teacher: ongoing negotiations across home-school boundaries', in M. David, R. Edwards, M. Hughes, and J. Ribbens (eds) *Mothers and Education: Inside Out? Exploring family-education policy and experience.* London: Macmillan

Robertson, S. (1996) 'Teachers' Work Re-structuring and Post-Fordism: constructing the new 'professionalism', In I. F. Goodson and A. Hargreaves (eds) *Teachers' Professional Lives.* London: Falmer

Rose, N. (1990) *Governing the Soul: the shape of the private self.* London: Routledge

Rose, N. (1996) 'Governing 'advanced' liberal democracies', in A. Barry, T .Osborne, and N. Rose (eds) *Foucault and Political Reason.* London: University College Press

Scott, G. (1990) 'Parents and Pre-School Services: issues of parental involvement'. *International Journal of Sociology and Social Policy* 10: 1 pp.1-13

Sharp, R. and Green, A. (1975) *Education and Social Control.* London: Routledge and Kegan Paul

Smith, D. E. (1988) *The Everyday World as Problematic: a feminist sociology.* Milton Keynes: Open University Press

Smith, D.E. (1998) 'The Underside of Schooling: restructuring, privatization and women's unpaid work', in A. Griffith and S. Schecter (eds) *Mothering, Educating and Schooling (special issues) Journal for a Just and Caring Education* 4: 1 pp.11-30

Strauss, A. and Corbin, J. (1990) *Basics of Qualitative Research: grounded theory procedures and techniques.* London: Sage

Thomas, A. and Dennison, B. (1991) 'Parental or Pupil Choice: who really decides in urban schools?' *Education Management and Administration* 19: 4 pp.243-51

Thomas, H. and Martin, J. (1996) *Managing Resources for School Improvement: creating a cost effective school.* London: Routledge

Thornton, K. (1999) 'Citizenship May Become Compulsory Post 16'. *Times Educational Supplement.* 28 May

Tomlinson, S. (1991) *Home-School Partnerships.* (Education and Training Paper No 7). London: Institute for Public Policy Research

Tomlinson, S. (1992) 'Disadvantaging the Disadvantaged: Bangladeshis and education in Tower Hamlets'. *British Journal of Sociology of Education.* 13: 4 pp.437-46

Topping, K. (1986) *Parents as Educators.* London: Croom Helm

Topping, K (1996) 'The Effectiveness of Family Literacy', in S. Wolfendale and K. Topping (Eds.) *Family Involvement in Literacy.* London: Cassell

Troyna, B. and Vincent, C. (1994) 'The Discourses of Social Justice'. Paper presented at the British Educational Research Association Annual Conference, Oxford.

Ulich, K. (1989) 'Eltern und Schuler: die Schule als Problem in der Familienerziehung'. *Zeitschrift fur Sozialisations Forschung und Erzietungssoziologie,* 9. pp.179-194

Usher, R. and Edwards, R. (1994) *Postmodernism and Education.* London: Routledge

Vincent, C. (1996) *Parents and Teachers: power and participation.* London: Falmer

Vincent, C. Martin, J. and Ranson, S. (2000) 'Little Polities': schooling , governance and parental participation'. Final Report to the Economic and Social Research Council

Vincent, C. (2000) *Including Parents? Education, citizenship and parental agency.* Buckingham: Open University Press

Walkerdine, V. and Lucey, H. (1989) *Democracy in the Kitchen: regulating mothers and socialising daughters.* London: Virago

Walford, G. (1994) *Choice and Equity in Education.* London: Cassell

Wallman, S. (1978) 'The Boundaries of 'Race': processes of ethnicity in England'. *Man* 13: 2 pp.200-17

Whitty, G. (1997a) Education Policy and the Sociology of Education. *International Studies in the Sociology of Education* 7: 2 pp.121-35

Whitty, G. (1997b) 'Marketization, the State and the Re-formation of the Teaching Profession', in A.H. Halsey, H. Lauder, P. Brown, and A. Stuart Wells (eds) *Education: culture, economy, society.* Oxford: Oxford University Press

Whitty, G., Power, S. and Halpin, D. (1998) *Devolution and Choice in Education: the school, the state and the market.* Buckingham: Open University Press

Willis, P. (1977) *Learning to Labour.* Farnborough, Hampshire: Saxon House

Wolfendale, S. (1992) *Empowering Parents and Teachers.* London: Cassell

Woodhead, C. (1999) *The Annual Report of Her Majesty's Chief Inspector of Schools: Standards and quality 1997/1998.* London: The Stationery Office

Woodhead, C. (2000) *The Annual Report of Her Majesty's Chief Inspector of Schools: Standards and quality 1998/1999.* London: The Stationery Office

Woods, P. (1993) 'Responding to the Consumer: parental choice and school effectiveness'. *School Effectiveness and School Improvement* 4: 3, pp.205-29

Woods, P. and Jeffrey, R. (1996) 'A New Professional Discourse? Adjusting to managerialism', in P. Woods (ed) *Contemporary Issues in Teaching and Learning.* London: Routledge, in association with the Open University Press

Wyness, M. (1997) 'Parental Responsibilities: Social policy and the maintenance of boundaries'. *The Sociological Review* 45 pp.304-24

Yeatman, A. (1994) *Postmodern Revisionings of the Political.* London, New York: Routledge

Young, I. M. (1989) 'Polity and Group Difference: a critique of the idea of universal citizenship'. *Ethics* 99 pp.250-74

Appendix 1

Details of Lowlands School

The school is a mixed 11-16 LEA-controlled school. It is situated in a semi-residential area, on the edge of a medium-sized town which has developed a number of high-tech industries and some car manufacturing. In spite of this, there is high unemployment in the area surrounding the school and many of the children's parents are without waged employment. According to the school's OFSTED report (1998), the school draws its students from an area which is marked by socio-economic deprivation. The number of students eligible for free school meals is above the national average at 31-35%. The report also describes the children's levels of literacy and numeracy on coming to the school as 'low'. The percentage of students with statements of special educational needs is 3.7% which is twice as high as the LEA average. The school describes its student population as emanating from mainly working-class backgrounds. The percentage of students gaining five or more A–C GCSE passes in 1998 was 13% compared to the national average of 43%; five or more A–G passes was 76% compared to the national average of 89%, and one or more A–G passes was 88% compared to the national average of 94%.

Appendix 2

Methodological details for the research at Lowlands School

A questionnaire survey was carried out at Lowlands School with 474 students from years 7, 8, 9 and 10. The questionnaire was distributed in tutor time by the group tutor. The question on parents' occupation was disliked by some students who did not feel comfortable replying to it. They were told that they did not have to answer questions that they did not want, or know how, to answer.

The questionnaire data were analysed using SNAP software. A baseline analysis was employed. In the following year the questionnaire survey was followed up with interviews of children from years 7 and 10.

Using a semi-structured interview, we interviewed 14 girls and 14 boys from year 7 and 20 girls and 20 boys from year 10: a total of 68. We interviewed them in single-sex groups, mixed-sex groups and on a one-to-one basis. As a warm-up activity we also asked them to complete a questionnaire to find out something about themselves and the sorts of things they might do at home with their parents. We distributed this ourselves and asked them to complete it in our presence. Following the completion of this questionnaire, we asked for students who would be interested in being interviewed. From their responses we made a random selection but did take into account the gender distribution.

All interviews were tape-recorded with the students' permission, and then transcribed; they lasted between 15 and 45 minutes. Anonymity was guaranteed and all names have been changed.

Appendix 3

Parents' social class and additional details

BRIGHTSIDE SCHOOL

NAME	SEX	OCCUPATION BASED ON HOPE-GOLDTHORPE 36 CATEGORY SCALE	CATEGORY BASED ON 7 FOLD CLASS SCHEMA	CLASS	EDUCATION	NO. OF CHILDREN	HOUSING
Bristow yr7	F	Deputy headteacher	Lower grade professional	II	Grammar school; university degree		
Bristow yr7	M	Social services manager	Lower grade administrator	II	State secondary but private primary school; university degree; PGCE social worker training	2 children at Brightside	Owner occupier
Brookes – yr7	F	Assistant housekeeper in hotel	Rank and file service worker	III	No qualifications	3 children 2 at Brightside	Owner occupier
Brookes yr7	M	Works for postal service	Semi-skilled worker in industry	VII	No data		
Brown yr7	F	Homeworker			Comprehensive school		
Brown yr7	M	Tenant Farmer	Small proprietor	IV	Comprehensive school; CSEs	2 children 1 at Brightside	Rented accommodation

Butler yr9	F	Looks after her family; was a solicitor	Self-employed professional	I	A levels; degree in law	3 children at Brightside	Owner occupier
Butler yr9	M	Senior lecturer at university	Higher grade professional	I	Degree		Owner occupier
Crook – yr11	F	Senior Clerk in university finance office	Routine non manual	III	Grammar school; 3 O levels and some CSEs	2 children at Brightside	Owner occupier
Crook Y11	M	Postperson	Semi-skilled manual	VI	Grammar school; no qualifications		
Darby yr11	F	Secondary teacher	Lower grade professional	II	Grammar school; 'A' levels; degree; PGCE		
Darby yr11	M	Sound engineer at BBC	Higher grade technician	II	Private school; I 'A' level	3 children 2 at Brightside	Owner occupier
Dorn yr11	F	Cleaner. Worked previously in shoe factory and as clerk for turf accountant	Unskilled manual	VII	Business studies course after leaving school	3 children 2 at Brightside	Owner occupier
Dorn yr11	M	Self-employed roofer	Self-employed artisan	IV	Grammar school; left education at 16		
Douglas yr11 Lone parent	F	Part time secretary/ proof reader/researcher	Routine non-manual Clerical	III	No data	3 children 1 at Brightside	Owner occupier
Dyer yr7	F	Cleaner	Unskilled manual	VII	No qualifications		
Dyer yr7	M	Builder/roofer	Semi-skilled manual worker	VI	Comprehensive school; 5yr apprenticeship in bookbinding	3 children 2 at Brightside	Local authority housing

NAME	SEX	OCCUPATION BASED ON HOPE-GOLDTHORPE 36 CATEGORY SCALE	CATEGORY BASED ON 7 FOLD CLASS SCHEMA	CLASS	EDUCATION	NO. OF CHILDREN	HOUSING
Foley yr11 Lone parent	F	School administrator/part time youth worker	Routine non-manual	III	No qualifications	3 children at Brightside	Owner occupier
Foster yr11	F	Homeworker			1 qualification in English from school	4 children 1 at Brightside	Local authority housing
Foster — yr11	M	Milkman	Unskilled manual worker	VII	No qualifications, left school at 15		
Hale yr11 Lone parent	F	General assistant in infant school	Routine non-manual	III	Girls' grammar school; university degree	3 children 2 at Brightside	Owner occupier
Henderson yr9	F	Counsellor for NSPCC. (was previously teacher)	Lower grade professional	II	B.Ed. Hons Degree	3 children 1 at Brightside	Owner occupier
Henderson yr9	M	Doctor	Higher grade professional	I	Medical degree		
Higgins — yr11	F	Teacher	Lower grade professional	II	'A' levels; teacher training	3 children 2 at Brightside	Owner occupier
Higgins yr11	M	Lecturer in higher education	Higher grade professional	I	Education up to Ph.D		

Name	Sex	Occupation	Class	Education	Children	Housing
Hill yr7	F	Secondary teacher	Lower grade professional	II	Girls' grammar school; Cert.Ed. recently upgraded to B.Ed.	2 children 1 at Brightside	Owner occupier
Hill yr7	M	Director of electronics firm.	Lower grade manager	II	Grammar school; HND in electrical engineering.		Owner occupier
Jones yr9	F	Student			Technical school; O levels; further education took A level sociology, typing, RSA word processing	2 children 1 at Brightside	Owner occupier
Jones yr9	M	Grid engineer for gas board	Higher grade technician	II	Grammar education. Now doing open university course.		
Land yr9	F	Unwaged homeworker			No qualifications	4 children 2 at Brightside	Owner occupier
Land yr9	M	Service engineer in oil industry	Skilled manual	VI	Comprehensive school; apprenticeship		
Lennox yr11	M	Structural design engineer	Higher grade professional	I	Direct grant school. Bsc in Civil engineering. Professional qualifications	2 children at Brightside	Owner occupier

NAME	SEX	OCCUPATION BASED ON HOPE-GOLDTHORPE 36 CATEGORY SCALE	CATEGORY BASED ON 7 FOLD CLASS SCHEMA	CLASS	EDUCATION	NO. OF CHILDREN	HOUSING
Lennox yr11	F	Social worker	Lower grade professional	II	Grammar school; degree; diploma in social work.		
Marchant yr7	F	Primary teacher	Lower grade professional	II	Grammar school; Degree;Cert.Ed	2 children at Brightside	Owner occupier
Marchant yr7	M	Chartered banker	Higher grade professional	I	Technical school		Owner occupier
Money yr7	F	Social worker	Lower grade professional	II	Grammar school, 3 A levels, sociology degree	3 children at Brightside	Owner occupier
Money yr7	M	Secondary teacher	Lower grade professional	II	Grammar school; 3 A levels; engineering degree; PGCE		
Rigg yr9	M	Self-employed architectural consultant	Self-employed professional	II	Architectural qualification	3 children 2 at Brightside	Owner occupier
Rigg yr9	F	General assistant in Primary school	Routine non-manual	III	Left school early to become secretary		
Ringston yr7	F	Previously worked as a secretary; now waiting to start a degree course			A levels; married instead of going to university	2 children 1 at Brightside	Owner occupier

Name	Sex	Occupation	Class	Category	Education	Children	Housing
Rington yr7	M	Sales manager for computer company	Lower grade manager	II	Left school after O levels and joined the army; trained on the job as computer programmer		
Robson yr9	F	Administrative officer at MOD	Routine non-manual	III	8 CSEs	3 children 2 at Brightside	Local authority housing
Robson yr9	M	Unskilled bookbinder (was previously skilled worker in engineering for 25 years)	Skilled manual	VI	No formal qualifications		
Shearer yr9	F	Clerical worker	Routine non-manual/ clerical	III	Private boarding school	3 children 2 at Brightside	Owner occupier
Shearer yr9	M	Quantity surveyor	Higher grade professional	I	Scholarship to public school; A levels; degree in building		
Skinner yr7	F	Artist (previously art teacher)	Self-employed professional	II	Comprehensive school; Art school.	2 children at Brightside	Owner occupier
Skinner yr7	M	Illustrator	Self-employed professional	II	Educated abroad; Higher education at architectural college		Owner occupier
Stewart yr7	F	School cleaner	Unskilled manual	VII	No qualifications	2 children at Brightside	Local authority housing

NAME	SEX	OCCUPATION BASED ON HOPE-GOLDTHORPE 36 CATEGORY SCALE	CATEGORY BASED ON 7 FOLD CLASS SCHEMA	CLASS	EDUCATION	NO. OF CHILDREN	HOUSING
Stewart yr7	M	Unemployed labourer	Unskilled manual	VII	No qualifications		
Thomas – yr11	F	Unemployed. Previous employment as lecturer	Higher grade professional	I	Degree as mature student	1 child at Brightside	Owner occupier
Wilson yr9	F	State registered nurse	Lower grade professional	II	Educated abroad; equivalent 'A' levels; nursing qualification	2 children 1 at Brightside	Owner occupier
Wilson yr9	M	Crane operator	Skilled manual worker in industry	VI	Equivalent of GCSEs		

ACRE LANE SCHOOL

NAME	SEX	OCCUPATION BASED ON HOPE-GOLDTHORPE 36 CATEGORY SCALE	CATEGORY BASED ON 7 FOLD CLASS SCHEMA	CLASS	EDUCATION	NO. OF CHILDREN	HOUSING
Bailey Y11 Lone parent	F	Clerical worker with BT	Clerical work	III	Comprehensive school, 10 O levels 4 A levels	3 children 1 at Acre Lane	Owner occupier
Banks Y9	F	Special needs classroom assistant	Routine non-manual	III	No data	3 children 2 at Acre Lane	Owner occupier
Banks Y9	M	Divisional officer in fire brigade	Lower grade official	II	3 O levels and 4 CSEs; took City and Guilds in printing; all subsequent professional qualifications in fire service		
Black Y11 Lone parent (Widow)	F	Sewing machinist – now she doesn't work	Skilled manual	VI	Secondary modern school, no qualifications; left at 15	1 child at Acre Lane	Owner occupier
Brown Y11 Lone parent	F	Part-time school meals assistant	Semi-skilled manual worker	VII	No qualifications	2 children 1 at Acre Lane	Local authority housing

NAME	SEX	OCCUPATION BASED ON HOPE-GOLDTHORPE 36 CATEGORY SCALE	CATEGORY BASED ON 7 FOLD CLASS SCHEMA	CLASS	EDUCATION	NO.OF CHILDREN	HOUSING
Falmer Y11 Lone parent	F	Registered General Nurse	Lower grade professional	II	Grammar school 2 CSEs Nurse training	2 children 1 at Acre Lane	Owner occupier
Falmer Y11 [ex husband]	M	Surveyor	Higher grade professional	I	Private School; 9 O levels 2 A levels ;Chartered surveyor		
Gale Y7	F	Auxilliary nurse in hospice; previously an office worker	Routine non manual	III	Girls' grammar school;'good grades' in 5 O levels.	2 children 1 at Acre Lane	Owner occupier
Gale Y7	M	Fire fighter	Lower grade technician	V	No qualifications apart from professional qualifications in fire service		
Horn Y7	F	Unwaged homeworker; helps in family business, unwaged			Comprehensive school; 1 O level in English and RSA typing; evening course in IT skills: CLAIT	2 children at Acre Lane	Owner occupier

	Sex	Occupation	Classification	Class	Education	Children	Housing
Horn Y7	M	Self-employed proprietor of coach company	Small proprietor	IV	Comprehensive school; 3 or 4 O levels		Owner occupier
Hoskins Y11	F	Insurance company clerical work; works part-time	Routine non-manual	III	Comprehensive school	2 children at Acre Lane	
Hoskins Y7	M	Works in computer department for a large insurance company	Manager in computer department	II	Private school; 1 A level; ONC computer programming course		
Hoyle Y9	F	State Registered Nurse	Lower grade professional	II	Comprehensive school	4 children; 2 at Acre Lane	Owner occupier
Hoyle Y9	M	Engineering consultant	Higher grade technician	II	Private school; 8 O levels, aeronautical engineering qualifications		
Lang Y7	F	Local council revenue officer	Lower grade administrator	III	Comprehensive, school: CSEs mainly, 2 O levels, City and Guilds beauty/hairdressing; BTEC in business and finance; doing Open University foundation course in social science	2 children at Acre Lane	Owner occupier

NAME	SEX	OCCUPATION BASED ON HOPE-GOLDTHORPE 36 CATEGORY SCALE	CATEGORY BASED ON 7 FOLD CLASS SCHEMA	CLASS	EDUCATION	NO. OF CHILDREN	HOUSING
Lang Y7	M	Mechanic	Lower grade technician	V	Comprehensive school; left with no qualifications; Later did an apprenticeship; Certificate of Professional Competence		
Laurel Y7	M	Mechanic	Lower grade technician	V	No qualifications	3 children 1 at Acre Lane	Owner occupier
Laurel Y7	F	Shop assistant	Routine non-manual	III	No qualifications		
McClelland	F	Part-time hairdresser	Self-employed	IV	Private school; 2 O levels	3 children 2 at Acre Lane	Owner occupier
McClelland Y9	M	Self-employed stonemason	Self employed artisan	IV	Private and state comprehensive schools; stonemason qualifications		
Milton Y11	F	Factory worker and works in canteen	Unskilled manual	VII	Comprehensive school; no qualifications	2 children 1 at Acre Lane	Local authority housing

	Sex	Occupation	Class description	Class	Education	Children	Housing
Milton Y11	M	Telephone engineer	Lower grade technicians	V	Comprehensive school; left without any qualifications; trained as a telephone engineer	3 children 1 at Acre Lane	Owner occupier
Mornington Y9	F	Unwaged homeworker			Secondary Modern; no qualifications		
Mornington Y9	M	Manager in postal delivery office	Supervisor of manual workers	V	Secondary modern school; no qualifications		
Moss Y9	F	No data			Secondary modern school; No qualifications	4 children at Acre Lane	Local authority housing
Moss Y9	M	Self-employed builder; has been in the army	Self-employed artisan	IV	3 O levels		
Parker Y11	M	Butcher	Skilled manual	VI	Comprehensive School; CSEs	2 children at Acre Lane	Owner occupier
Parker Y11	F	Unwaged homeworker; was shop assistant; occasionally does some child-minding	Routine non-manual	III	No qualifications		
Price Y7	F	Unwaged homeworker; helps in family business, unwaged			Comprehensive school; no qualifications	3 children 2 at Acre Lane	Owner occupier
Price Y7	M	Self-employed	Self-employed artisan	IV	Comprehensive school; 1 O level in mathematics		

NAME	SEX	OCCUPATION BASED ON HOPE-GOLDTHORPE 36 CATEGORY SCALE	CATEGORY BASED ON 7 FOLD CLASS SCHEMA	CLASS	EDUCATION	NO.OF CHILDREN	HOUSING
Pye Y7	F	Administrator for family business – private shiatsu school	Self-employed clerical.	III	State coed boarding school; O levels; F.E. college for economics, accounts and secretarial qualifications	4 children 2 at Acre Lane	Owner occupier
Pye Y7	M	Owns and manages private shiatsu school	Self-employed professional/teacher	II	Private boarding school; Psychology hons degree; PGCE		
Reading Y9 Lone parent	F	No occupation at present; did work in a bank after school.	Routine clerical	III	Left school in fifth year to work in a bank.	5 children 2 at Acre Lane	Local authority housing
Stanley Y11	F	Homeworker; was a factory worker, then worked in factory office, then sales assistant in food hall	Routine non manual	III	Comprehensive school, left with no qualifications	3 children 2 at Acre Lane	Owner occupier
Stanley Y11 [step father]	M	Lorry driver	Semi-skilled manual	VII	Comprehensive school; no qualifications		
Stores Y7	F	Part-time Administrative officer	Routine clerical	III	Comprehensive school, 4 O levels; 1 year in 6th form; did sociology A level recently.	1 child at Acre Lanes	Owner occupier

	Sex	Job	Occupation	Class	Education	Children	Housing
Stores Y7	M	Executive officer in civil service	Lower grade administrator	II	Grammar school		
Sweep Y9	F	Clerical worker at BT	Routine non-manual	III	Grammar school; Took a diploma after leaving school	3 children 1 at Acre Lane	Owner occupier
Sweep Y9	M	Maintenance worker	Skilled manual worker	VI	Technical college; City and Guilds in planning		
Tasker Y9 Lone Parent	F	Part-time temporary secretary	Routine clerical	III	4 O levels	6 children 2 at Acre Lane	Local authority housing
Webb Y9	F	Secretary	Routine non-manual, clerical	III	State boarding school, 3 O levels, 5 CSEs	2 children at Acre Lane	Owner Occupier
Webb Y9	M	Lorry fitter	Skilled manual	VI	Attended a special school; no qualifications		
Woodside Y11	F	Factory work; now unemployed due to illness	Unskilled manual	VII	Secondary modern girls' school; no qualifications	5 children 2 at Acre Lane	Local authority housing
Woodside Y11	M	Unemployed; has done variety of jobs – postman, bus driver	Skilled manual	VI	Secondary modern school; no qualifications		

Index